MEDDICC

The ultimate guide to staying one step ahead in the complex sale

ANDY WHYTE

With foreword and commentary from MEDDIC co-creators Dick Dunkel and Jack Napoli

DEDICATION

To my wife, Katie, and my sons Charlie and Hugo. You are my world and Inspiration for everything I do.

To my brother, James. Your courage, bravery, and above all positivity in life is my inspiration to be a better person.

ACKNOWLEDGMENTS

To say this book is "by Andy Whyte" overstates the case. Without the ingenuity of Dick Dunkel to leverage the expertise of PTC leaders like John McMahon and encapsulate it into MEDDIC. For Dick and Jack Napoli to then have the gumption and confidence to go on a global tour, which ultimately resulted in the proliferation of MEDDIC to every corner of the globe - then there would be no book because there would be no MEDDIC.

Therefore, it is Dick Dunkel, Jack Napoli, and John McMahon, for whom I owe the most prominent acknowledgment.

Further still, Dick, Jack, and Steve Ammann's warmth, guidance, and expertise towards me from our earliest conversations gave me courage, confidence, and a renewed inspiration to work towards completing this book.

To Cliff Payne, my first sales manager, you gave me my start in sales, and while many may not credit door-to-door double-glazing sales, I learned more about the art and science of sales and, above all else, the importance of work ethic from you than I have anybody else since.

To Paola White, the first person to overlook my lack of B2B sales experience by giving me a shot as an SDR while also giving me the flexibility to grow into an Account Executive.

To Patrick Donnelly, who was the first entrepreneur I got to work for (he will hate me for calling him that). I learned so much about what it is to have 'nous' (Greek: nous, meaning intellect, or common sense) from you. The hustle from our early days of building ES Tech Group showed me that anything is possible with drive, creativity, and commitment.

Without Ragy Thomas, Carlos Dominguez, and Mike Logan, I wouldn't have had the opportunity to learn all of what I did at Sprinklr and benefit from the career projection altering effects of Force Management training delivered by John Kaplan and his team.

Without my sales peers and those that drove me to become a better individual contributor and sales leader - your coachability, curiosity, creativity, and the respect you show to the craft of sales inspired me to aim higher.

Finally, without the customers whose complex businesses and even more complex sales cycles kept me in a constant state of unease, and, therefore, always searching for answers, thank you! I never felt gratitude for you at the time, but with every uncertain engagement, I strived towards achieving more certainty in future engagements, which powered my enthusiasm to embrace MEDDICC.

All of this is to say that I see myself as merely a vessel of a combination of wonderful opportunities. I take it as a great honor that I get to bestow my experiences to you, the reader, so it is you who I would like to pass on my final acknowledgment – thank you for your trust in me by purchasing this book.

CONTENTS

FOREWORD

Dick Dunkel
"The Creator of MEDDIC":

Despite the incredible evolution of enterprise technology and the business world on the whole, it is perhaps surprising that a methodology born over 25 years ago could still be enthusiastically implemented with such momentum as MEDDICC is today.

On the other hand, when you consider the circumstances formed as the nucleus for its creation, maybe it's not surprising at all.

The story of MEDDICC has many beginnings.

For me, it started with a college experience that reflected a restless sense of (or perhaps lack of) direction involving rugby, two summers selling books door to door, and an Engineering degree. Graduation was followed by a short stint as a design engineer, but I quickly grew restless for competition and self-determination. As the offspring of 2 self-made salespeople, dad sold advertising space for Sports Illustrated and Time Inc. (think Mad Men), and mom wore a hard hat and sold site remediation services (think hazardous waste), I felt it was inevitable.

I made the quantum leap into what would be the first step in a long sales career and spent the next six years selling for Xerox Corporation and Xerox Engineering Systems. Xerox deservedly had an excellent reputation for training and development. Neil Rackham's "SPIN Selling" was central to helping

Xerox sellers understand and develop customer needs. Learning to apply this simple framework was foundational to my success and would influence how I organized my own ideas about the key to sales success.

Following those productive years at Xerox, I felt ready for a new challenge and became aware of PTC while exploring new opportunities. I secured the interview, and during the process, I remember having the distinct feeling that I was graduating to the big leagues of competitive enterprise selling. Grittier, faster moving, high accountability, powerful, highly differentiated offering, strong leadership top to bottom. I did not see a weak link, and if it existed, it was identified and either fixed or removed quickly. PTC was an organization on a mission and required total commitment. It was an intense experience to be a part of. I spent two years as a sales representative selling Pro-Engineer to manufacturers, suppliers, and fabricators in Eastern PA.

In early 1996, I received an unexpected call from PTC's head of sales development, Anne Gary. Anne reported to John McMahon, who was the SVP of Sales. I was invited to go to PTC HQ in Waltham, MA, to do a stint on the Sales Development team. (PTC leveraged the Sales Development program to develop future leaders.) John and Anne were looking for someone to develop a new Intermediate Sales Training class that would be part of their "5 Touches Plan." The plan was to institute five development touches during the first year to accelerate learning, increase sales performance, and reduce turnover.

I accepted the position, and in the Spring of 1996, our small family (wife Carolyn, who was seven months pregnant, and two-year-old son Timothy) moved to Mass. where we rented a small house in Needham.

Under John and Anne's direction, and with support from teammates Dale Monnin and Jack Napoli, the new Intermediate Sales Training course was developed. This new course was designed for PTC sellers who had already completed New Hire training and had several months of in-field experiences that they were expected to share during this new class.

During this class, we conducted an exercise (that I still do today with various sales teams) called:

Why Do We Win? Why Do We Lose? Why Do Deals Slip?

During this exercise, the class would list all their answers, and then those answers would be bundled based on common themes.

After running the exercise several times, the recurring themes were emerging, with some regional differences. Different teams were highlighting different priorities based on the direction their regional sales leaders had given them. I remember thinking at the time that this was something worth standardizing on.

What would we do with it? How would we use it? I have to confess, this was not fully baked in my mind yet, but I was pretty sure we had "something."

I shared the six recurring themes with John and suggested that we establish them as our essential building blocks for sales success.

John agreed, and MEDDIC was born.

No consultants, no science projects. Just sales guys collecting inputs from real-world experiences and establishing a useful framework that would help us to drive consistency in communication, qualification, and execution.

With John's support, we began embedding MEDDIC into our sales training and qualification process.

That Fall, Jack Napoli and I went on a world tour to drive MEDDIC adoption throughout PTC.

The next four years at PTC focused on upskilling the Account Executives to help us drive towards the magic goal of $1billion of revenue.

Our journey from $300m to over $1bn revenue took just four years, and along those four years, PTC met and exceeded every quarterly revenue goal in front of them.

The early 2000s saw a massive expansion of the tech landscape. With that expansion came opportunities for the legions of sales leaders that McMahon and other executives at PTC had groomed.

McMahon would lead sales at Ariba, BladeLogic, and then BMC and advise many great sales-driven organizations, including AppDynamics, HubSpot, Fuze, and Sumo Logic, Sprinklr, and ThinkSpot.

Jack would begin his journey as the person perhaps most responsible for the proliferation of and adoption of MEDDIC with technology companies worldwide.

John Kaplan, who started as a District Manager for PTC in North Carolina, and would go on to lead PTC sales organizations in Europe, and Grant Wilson, who led PTC sales teams in the Americas and Asia and ran Global Sales Ops, joined forces to create Force Management, a successful sales transformation consultancy.

There are so many others who have been Champions of MEDDIC and have leveraged its lasting principles to drive success for their organizations and their customers.

> *I'll never forget the first time I presented MEDDIC in class after doing our "Win-Lose-Slip" exercise. It was July 1996, give or take a month. One of the new sales reps considered the six-letter acronym, then paused and said: "You mean to tell me that "I" is for Pain? That's the worst acronym I've ever heard." Everyone laughed. 2 weeks later, I got a call from that same sales rep who said: "Hey, I just wanted to tell you... I use MEDDIC all day, every day. I'll never forget it."*

Today it's hard to find a high-performing technology sales organization that doesn't have heritage linking back to PTC; in fact, it is via this heritage that I came to know the author of this book, Andy.

I joined Sprinklr in 2015 and was reunited with John McMahon, who was on Sprinklr's board at the time. Sprinklr's Global Head of Sales Mike Logan (PTC 1995 - 99) and I agreed that I would join initially as an Account Executive to learn the business and then transition to lead Sales Enablement to support the planned growth of the organization.

Andy joined Sprinklr as an Account Executive a few months after me. We experienced working with MEDDPICC at Sprinklr from a reasonably casual perspective; it was still in its early adoption stages.

Mike Logan had overseen such momentous growth that Sprinklr had broken the much-lauded T2-D3 model where "hot" SaaS companies see their size "triple, triple, double, double, and double," Sprinklr had tripled three years in a row. To support the growth plan, I transitioned from the field and returned to my passion for sales development. To accelerate delivery and adoption at scale, Mike turned to Force Management. Together we drove the adoption of MEDDPICC and our value messaging framework.

During this time, I got to know Andy and immediately recognized that he was "all in." Andy embraced the key concepts and, through his leadership, helped the broader UK team do the same. After Sprinklr, Andy went into another individual contributor role where he had to rely on his discipline to use MEDDICC before stepping into sales leadership where he has since implemented MEDDICC into two organization's he has led as well as advising the implementation of MEDDICC to seed-funded startups through to Series D and E SaaS companies. Through these experiences, I've come to see that Andy is truly a "student of sales," steadily accumulating knowledge and perspective, which you'll find in these pages. His diverse, hands-on experiences have provided Andy with a unique perspective that you, the reader, can benefit from in this book.

MEDDICC has enjoyed the success it has had because a) it's based on timeless principles and b) it's practitioners are not in the "ivory tower," but instead they are "in the arena." Rank matters not. AE, Manager, AVP, SVP, CRO, those who embrace MEDDICC are "in the field" because selling is in their blood, and they are on a mission to unlock value for their customers.

Fortunately for us, we finally have a proven leader and a true student of sales in Andy, who has taken the time away from the front line to document it.

When Andy told me about his plan to utilize the time he was saving on his commute due to COVID19 to write this book, I was very excited and was honored when Andy asked me to write the foreword.

I am confident you will benefit from the pearls of wisdom within this book, regardless of whether you are part of the PTC originals that Jack and I trained, right through to someone who is picking up this book with no former MEDDICC experience.

Whether you are an individual contributor or sales leader, my advice is that you should start to implement MEDDICC into what you do straight away. Embrace MEDDICC, and you and your team will more clearly understand the WHY to your process, and you'll begin to execute your customer interactions with more purpose and achieve better results.

And like so many others before, you will begin to reap the rewards of having a well-qualified pipeline of opportunities with clearer paths to success.

Dick Dunkel

Jack Napoli –
"The Godfather of MEDDIC":

It is a pleasure and a privilege to have been asked to write this Foreword for Andy's book on MEDDICC.

I struggled in sales, and just like how Andy thought he was an A-Player until he found MEDDICC, I had the same experience when I joined Parametric Technology Corporation, better known as PTC.

I recall it like it was yesterday "They are so lucky to have me – I have 10 years of software sales experience". However, after about 2 weeks, I realized just how far away from the standard I was. I didn't have 10 years' experience; I had 1 year of experience repeated 10 times.

What lay ahead of me in the next 74 quarters at PTC would be the most transformative period of not just my 40-year enterprise sales career but also that of enterprise sales itself as PTC was about to embark on the most meteoric run of growth ever seen technology sales.

I was PTC's 32nd employee and only the 4th Salesperson. Within my time at PTC, we grew to over 800 Sellers and more than 5,500 employees. I am proud to say I spent 74 quarters at PTC.

I only ever refer to time within PTC via the measure of quarters; this is because, in Enterprise Sales, nobody cares what kind of year you are going to have. It's all about your Quarter. To paraphrase what our Leadership team of CEO Steve Walske, CRO Dick Harrison, and VP of Worldwide Sales Mike McGuiness espoused at the time: "Longevity with the company has nothing to do with Future Employment." PTC was a true Meritocracy.

This results-focused environment cultivated by the leadership team laid the perfect foundation for a methodology like MEDDIC to be created, and while I am often referred to as the

'Godfather' of MEDDIC, a nickname I enjoy, it is Dick Dunkel who is the "biological" Father as it was Dick that codified it into the acronym we know and love today.

MEDDIC was the combination of John McMahon's brilliant sales mind and Dick Dunkel's creativity. Once Dick had documented it, and he and I implemented it at PTC, he, Pete Tyrell, and I embarked on a worldwide 17 city Demo Tour and sowed the MEDDIC seeds along with every sales manager in the company at the time.

I also used the methodology when I managed direct sales reps working for PTC and members of our Channel Program. It was my "guide" to meet the reps where they were in their skillset and coach them up to where they were aspiring to be.

The role in which I used MEDDIC the most was when I was a VP of Customer Care. This role was very much a precursor to our SaaS world today, and my team and I looked after the existing customer base. One thing started to become apparent to me, though I never got to meet the "happy" customers. I was only sent in when the "value proposition" didn't meet the expectations set out.

With MEDDIC as our guide, we were able to put unhappy customers on a path towards success. One time we took a customer who had spent a grand total of $140,000 in 7 years to increase their spend by over 800% within the next year. We credited the majority of this success to MEDDIC.

Of my 36 Quota carrying quarters at PTC, I participated in eight Presidents Clubs. But, the one year I missed Presidents Club was where I learned the most. From that experience and all of my experiences surrounded by the "sea of talent" at PTC, I became a lifelong learner.

I look upon this honor that Andy shared with me to author the Foreword of this book as an opportunity to help you, the reader, Andy the Author, and myself on my quest for Continuous Improvement.

I was introduced to Andy by Dick Dunkel. I heard of his lineage at SaaS start-ups and established players like Sprinklr.

When I learned he had been working with Dick and received in-depth training from Force Management, it validated what I value, which is a visceral commitment to MEDDIC. You see, like MEDDIC itself, which was documented "by salespeople for salespeople," Andy lives in the same "White Hot" selling environment and is fresh from battle where in his day job, Andy is driving Revenue, Profitability, and a Pipeline for a technology company.

Who better to learn from?

I would love to tell you I'm the best sales trainer in the world. The reality is the best person to educate someone who is doing a job like sales is: Someone else that is selling like Andy is.

I'll hold my own when it comes to sales leadership experience and sales education; however, when I see the passion, commitment, and desire to improve from someone like Andy, I'm in – All in.

There is something here for everyone, which is what captured my imagination. When I saw how Andy covered not only MEDDIC but some of the ancillary methodologies that when appropriately used to work "frictionlessly" to advance your opportunities.

Perhaps you are a well-educated MEDDICC Elite Enterprise Seller looking for an edge, or you have been newly introduced to MEDDICC more casually.

Whether you are an Elite Seller with years of experience using MEDDICC right across the spectrum of expertise to being brand new to it, you will find valuable information within this book.

Regardless of whether you are a Seller, a Sales Leader, in Pre-Sales, Post-Sales, Marketing, or Customer Success, the "Common Language" of MEDDICC will benefit you.

Good selling, and I trust you'll enjoy the journey that Andy will take us on.

Jack Napoli

PREFACE

Before I learned MEDDICC, I would rate myself firmly as a B-Player salesperson. At the time, I'd have stated that I was striving to be an A-Player. I genuinely had no idea just how far away I was from being an A-Player as nobody had lifted the veil of what I was missing by not tapping into a qualification methodology like MEDDICC.

My first interaction with any form of MEDDICC came at Sprinklr. On the week-long onboarding session at their New York City HQ, my fellow Sprinklrites and I were taken through what MEDDPICC was and how Sprinklr used it. However, upon returning to Europe, it was rarely referenced again.

It wasn't until we were recalled to America for a training course with Force Management that MEDDPICC would be taken more seriously in Europe, wherein coalition with Force Management's game-changing 'Command of the Message' value framework, my approach to sales would never be the same again.

After Sprinklr came a SaaS company called Tealium, where, once again, MEDDICC was covered in onboarding a similar amount of detail to Sprinklr, but just like Sprinklr, upon returning to Europe, it was seldom referenced again. The only remnant of its existence being the empty MEDDICC fields within the opportunity page on Salesforce.

My next challenge came at Poq, a Series A SaaS company with just under $3m ARR, where I was brought in to help 'enterprise up' the sales team.

An anecdote that gives insight into the task I had ahead of me was that on my first forecast call, a Seller for Poq was asked whether the close date for a deal in question was still set for the end of the month, which was merely two weeks away. The Seller responded affirmatively and confidently stated:

> *"I haven't heard back from them for a couple of weeks now, but they have been opening my emails a lot so I am still pretty confident we are on track."*

Needless to say, the deal went on to be lost as we never heard from the customer again.

Going into Poq, I knew there would be several initiatives I could deploy to 'enterprise' them up. Still, it was immediately apparent that MEDDICC would be the most beneficial.

2018 saw Poq targeting increasing its overall Annual Recurring Revenue (ARR) by 160%. This is an extremely challenging task for any SaaS company, especially one with questionable product-market fit within a vertical market such as retail. To achieve the target, we needed to have a relentless focus on qualification by ensuring all of the steps of MEDDICC you are going to read about within this book were adhered to closely.

MEDDICC provided the perfect methodology for this enhancement. I believe it was the main contributing factor to how Poq was able to achieve 103% of the 2018 target and forecast within a margin of 10% for each quarter.

The next challenge for me came with the opportunity to lead the EMEA team for a company called Branch, a Series E startup in Silicon Valley. The task at Branch wasn't too dissimilar to Poq in that the team needed to qualify better. Still, there was also an added challenge where the EMEA region was radically underperforming compared to the North America region, where they saw deal sizes over 120% higher, and their conversion rate was also 86% higher.

We implemented MEDDICC immediately. At the time of writing this chapter (9 months later), the average order value in EMEA has doubled. We have also reduced the average sales cycle length by 30%, which is a very unusual achievement.

Typically, as deal values rise, so does the time taken to close them.

Four out of the top five Branch customers in EMEA have been won since the implementation of MEDDICC, and if the current forecast is to be believed, then by the first anniversary of implementing MEDDICC, only one of the top ten most valuable customers in EMEA will all have been won before we implemented MEDDICC.

I love MEDDICC. As an individual contributor, it acted as a map that helped me get to the point of decision in a predictive manner. It shone a light on an otherwise dark journey. As a sales leader, it has helped me drive predictable and accurate forecasts into sales teams and to bring forecastable consistency across groups of salespeople who vary in optimism, style, and approach.

While I am proud of my success with MEDDICC, it loses significance when you consider how it has empowered some of the worlds' most elite sales organizations to drive hundreds of billions of dollars' worth of revenue.

INTRODUCTION

MEDDIC was born inside PTC in the 90s by Dick Dunkel. PTC is renowned as one of the most successful software companies of all time, and much of the credit is given to their sales team who took PTC from 0-10bn dollars in 10 years, which is a feat only surpassed by how they never missed a single quarterly target in over 43 straight targets—almost 11 years!

However, it wasn't always smooth sailing at PTC. When they were at around 300 Sellers, the attrition of Sellers became a real problem and PTC couldn't hire as quickly as they were losing Sellers. Something needed to change and a major factor in that change was to bring Dick Dunkel and Jack Napoli out of the field to revamp the new hire sales training program. As part of this process, Jack and Dick reviewed hundreds of opportunities and discovered that when they won, they dominated in six specific areas. They could also pinpoint a loss to one of these six areas too. These six areas would go on to be labeled: Metrics, Economic Buyer, Decision Criteria, Decision Process, Identify Pain, and Champion. This would, of course, therefore be known by the acronym MEDDIC.

PTC's relentless focus on qualification and its development of the MEDDIC methodology spawned thousands of MEDDIC proficient Sellers into the wider workforce. Today, if you look at some of the world's most successful sales leaders, you can trace their sales ancestry back to PTC.

The chart below shows the humongous impact PTC and their people's expertise have had on the enterprise technology landscape today:

What is MEDDICC?

MEDDICC is a Qualification Methodology that is widely adopted by the world's most elite sales organizations.

It is my belief that MEDDICC's strength comes in both its simplicity and depth. You can introduce MEDDICC to help you qualify your deal at the earliest opportunity and it stays relevant throughout its evolution keeping Sellers on their toes to focus on what matters.

MEDDICC is uniquely suited to enterprise sales organizations. Enterprise sales usually requires engagement with multiple stakeholders and often will require a complex solution to meet their needs. For this purpose, MEDDICC is ideally suited as a qualification methodology.

Why Do You Need a Qualification Methodology?

Sales leadership teams are trying to create predictable revenue for their execs, board members, and shareholders. There are two critical factors required to create predictable revenue:

1. Efficient Resource Allocation
2. Forecast Accuracy

Let's dive a little deeper into each:

1. Efficient Resource Allocation

Sellers and their supporting peers are often the highest-paid individuals within their organization. This is for good reason as an elite Seller is likely to deliver exponentially more revenue than what their additional cost is over an average Seller.

A Seller who is unable to qualify their opportunities won't just be inefficient to themselves, but they will also pull in other resources draining their efficiency too.

MEDDICC helps Sellers continually ensure that they are investing their time in the right deals, and if not, it gives a clear path of how they can get back on the right course or qualify out.

2. Forecast Accuracy

Being able to accurately forecast revenue performance allows organizations to confidently invest in strategies that support growth such as hiring to support the growing customer base and investing more in go-to-market strategies.

For the executive team, being able to work with an accurate forecast is imperative to their planning and execution.

Elite Sellers are accurate forecasters and elite sales leaders are too.

MEDDICC Also Helps Your Customers

Customers who are buying from a sales organization that utilizes MEDDICC also benefit from an approach that is optimized to be efficient. It means that it won't just save the Seller's time but the customer's time too. Further still, the customer will benefit from a Seller focused on providing deeper clarity on the problem that the customer is trying to find a solution for. In doing so, the Seller will uncover a deeper quantification of the problem and potentially more benefits that the customer hadn't yet considered.

Finally, the cherry on top will be that a good Seller will help the customer drive a deal through their organization securing budget and buy-in as they go, cutting the time to go-live considerably.

MEDDIC? MEDDICC? MEDDPICC? MEDDPICCR?

There are multiple variants of the MEDDICC acronym, such as adding an additional D and C as well as a P and an R.

Selecting the right elements of the MEDDICC acronym for you will depend on your organization's structure. In my sales team, we implement MEDDPICCR to include the Paper Process and Risks as separate elements. From my research, the most commonly implemented variant is MEDDICC but that usually has the Paper Process included within the Decision Process. However, many new implementations of MEDDICC use MEDDPICC as their acronym.

MEDDIC with one C was the original acronym but is very rarely used in modern sales organizations.

Whichever you implement or follow will be a choice you have to make. For clarity, this book will solely refer to the methodology as 'MEDDICC' but will cover every letter of MEDDPICCR in full.

One of the wonderful things about MEDDICC is that since its creation decades ago, it has gone on to flourish across thousands of sales organizations. As it has expanded and grown, so too has the way people define it. I have seen the P be used for Partners, and a C used for Compelling Event. This book contains my definition of MEDDICC which correlates closely to the majority of instances I have seen it.

Do I think the exact definition of this book will represent MEDDICC in 5 or 10 years? I hope not!

What Do the Letters Stand For?

The letters are articulated as follows:

M is for Metrics: The Metrics are the quantifiable measures of value that your solution can provide.

E is for Economic Buyer: The Economic Buyer is the person with the overall authority in the buying decision.

D is for Decision Criteria: The Decision Criteria are the various criteria in which a decision to process your solution will be judged.

D is for Decision Process: The Decision Process is the series of steps that form a process of which the buyer will follow to make a decision.

P is for Paper Process: The Paper Process is the series of steps that follow the Decision Process in how you will go from Decision to signed contract.

I is for Implicate the Pain: Implicating the Pain means you have both Identified, Indicated, and Implicated the Pain your solution solves upon your customer.

C is for Champion: The Champion is a person who has power, influence, and credibility within the customer's organization.

C is for Competition: The Competition is any person, vendor, or initiative competing for the same funds or resources you are.

R is for Risks: The Risks are the specific Risks that you have identified within your deal that will either remain and need to be monitored or overcome.

Strap Yourself In

Whether you are a MEDDICC veteran from the days of its inception over twenty five years ago or this is your first introduction to MEDDICC, I assure you this book will be packed full of gems of information that you will find valuable.

Let's start!

HOW TO READ THIS BOOK

Throughout this book, I will refer to many different stakeholders and stages.

Some stakeholders, such as the Elite Seller, Champion, and Economic Buyer, play significant roles, whereas others, such as the Users and Procurement, play a smaller role. In contrast, the stages stay pretty consistent throughout the Early, Mid, and Late Stages.

Starting the book with a firm definition of the stakeholders and stages will provide much clarification and context to maximize your understanding of the contents of this book.

Note: To enhance the readability of this book, I generally refer to stakeholders in a singular format, even if there are likely to be multiple versions of the same stakeholder or, as is sometimes the case, a stakeholder consists of a committee of people.

Customer-Sided Stakeholders

The Customer

Everything should start with the customer, and this book is no different.

Within this book, the customer is the person or organization that is the buying party. They can be both a prospective and existing customer to the Seller.

The Solution Provider

The Solution Provider is the organization that is looking to sell its solution to the customer. You work for a solution provider.

Coach

The Coach is helpful towards the Seller and gives useful information. However, they are either not qualified to be a Champion, or the Seller has yet to test whether they measure up to be a Champion.

Champion

A Champion is a person who has power, influence, and credibility within the customer's organization. They have been qualified as someone who is both helping us by giving us useful information and selling internally for us. They also need to have a personal interest in the success of our deal.

Economic Buyer

The Economic Buyer is the overall authority in which the budget for your deal rolls up to. They are generally more senior executives and are focused on the high-level business outcomes of your deal.

They are known as the person who can say "No" when other people say "Yes", and vice versa.

Technical Buyer

The Technical Buyer is the technical authority on your deal. Their approval is usually required for your deal to pass the technical elements of the Decision Criteria.

Users

Users are the people who will be using your solution from day-to-day. They are often in the sales process in the early stages and can form part of the committee that decides and evaluates your solution against the Decision Criteria.

They are rarely influential in aspects outside of the technical suitability of your product. Their influence on this aspect of the Decision Criteria shouldn't be overlooked.

Procurement

Procurement has a very straightforward job, which is to ensure that the organization they work for gets the very best value from anything they buy.

They are often misunderstood as being the department that wants you to lower your price. However, if you approach them armed with a strong Champion and business case, you should find your engagement far more amicable than anticipated by their reputation.

Legal/Lawyers

In enterprise sales, it is highly unusual for two organizations to reach an agreement without the engagement of the legal departments.

The legal department works on everything from the NDA (Non-Disclosure Agreement) through to the Master Agreements and contracts.

Seller-Sided Stakeholders

The Seller

The Seller is the salesperson acting on behalf of The Solution Provider.

Sellers' job titles will vary from Account Executive and Sales Executive to more glamorous titles such as Sales Director and Regional Sales Manager.

They are usually measured and targeted by the amount of revenue they can close.

The Elite Seller

Elite Sellers are salespeople with the highest skillset, talent, and work ethic. There is a chapter detailing what defines an Elite Seller coming up.

The Sales Leader

An individual within The Solution Provider's organization whose role it is to manage the sales team.

The Stages of the Sales Process

While some enterprise sales organizations have similar sales processes, there are always nuances, and it is scarce to find two organizations with the same process. Therefore, in the interest of making the advice as applicable as possible within this book, we have broken the sales stages down into three stages: Early, Mid, and Late.

The Early-Stage

The early stages refer to the initial stages of your deal. The common elements of the early stages of the sales process are around qualification and discovery.

The Mid-Stage

The mid-stages of the sales process usually shift towards the presentation of value with proposals and business cases being the focus.

Sellers should be looking to validate that they match up against the Decision Criteria at this stage.

The Late-Stage

Depending on how the sales process is defined in your organization, you will either have the engagements with procurement, legal, and the related negotiations as of the late part of the mid-stage or early parts of the late-stage before it progresses to managing the close and the Paper Process.

IS MEDDICC A METHODOLOGY?

A frequently asked question is, "Is MEDDICC a Sales Methodology?" The short answer is "no," but it's not as straightforward as that as, over time, the lines of definition have blurred.

A sales methodology is a set of guiding principles that an organization uses to define how they go to market with their solution.

In its natural form, MEDDICC does not dictate the approach an organization should take in their go-to-market. MEDDICC provides a methodology in which the organization can correctly and thoroughly qualify deals to ensure efficient and effective selling. Therefore, MEDDICC is a Qualification Methodology.

You may think this is a little pedantic, but it is critical for the success of how people embrace MEDDICC that they don't make these two common mistakes:

1. Assuming that MEDDICC is a sales methodology and, therefore, will provide how their organization structures their go-to-market with such initiatives like product and value messaging.

2. Disregarding the opportunity to implement MEDDICC because they already have a Sales Methodology in place.

The mistake of assuming you can't implement MEDDICC because you already have a sales methodology is incorrect and overlooks one of the most valuable tenets of MEDDICC: it is wholly universal and works with the sales methodology. In fact, some sales methodologies are built upon MEDDICC, and, need MEDDICC to underpin them.

In enterprise sales, the sales methodology is Batman leading the attack, and MEDDICC is Robin, the trusty sidekick keeping everything on track and in check.

The sales methodology will lead on how your organization goes to market, the style of messaging, who you talk to, and how you speak to them.

If you were hoping that MEDDICC would act as a sales methodology for you, don't be disappointed; instead, be elated, you see, by implementing MEDDICC, you are going to accelerate your understanding of which sales methodology is right for your organization.

How to Choose the Right Methodology for your organization

There are several different types sales methodologies and providers, a few that you may be familiar with are below:

1. Sales MEDDIC Group
2. Force Management
3. SPIN Selling
4. The Sandler Selling Method
5. The Challenger Sale
6. Target Account Selling
7. Value Selling
8. Miller Heiman

There are three things you should do when selecting a sales methodology for your organization:

1. Find the Methodology that Best Suits Your Go-To-Market

The right sales methodology for you will depend on the solution you offer and your customer type.

If you are selling a mature type of solution where your customers already understand their problem and know how you can help solve them, then the majority of sales methodologies will work for your organization.

However, if the customer doesn't understand their problem or how your solution can help, or if they don't even know they have a problem, then the type of sales methodology becomes a more detailed decision.

This means that when you engage with prospective providers of sales methodologies, you should be looking for them to understand your organization, the needs of your customers, and how your value proposition helps.

2. Ensure it is Rigorously Implemented

For a sales methodology to be effective, it must be rigorously implemented in your organization.

The best sales methodology implementations I've seen looked like this:

Discovery Process - Methodology provider goes deep to understand the pains, goals, and challenges (they practice what they preach!).

Workshops - They surface what they have learned in workshops with key stakeholders within the organization to flesh out their understanding of the proposition and how it should be capsulized into the methodology.

Delivery - This is your traditional training course. Best in person with lots of practical exercises.

Embedding - The most important and yet most overlooked part of any methodology implementation is ensuring it is applied consistently and reinforced regularly.

The methodology must form a part of a universal language that guides your organization's sales activities, and it must be supported throughout the business from top to bottom and, in particular, with middle managers who are often under-invested in despite them having the most significant impact on the adoption rate.

Ensure It Is MEDDICC Compatible

The world's fastest-growing and most successful enterprise solution providers use MEDDICC to complement their sales methodology. If your sales methodology forces you to revert away from MEDDICC, the chances are it's doing so at the detriment of your ability to qualify.

MEDDICC VERSUS OTHER QUALIFICATION METHODOLOGIES

N ow we have established that MEDDICC is a qualification methodology, how does it compare against others?

The first thing to note is that MEDDICC is different from most qualification methodologies for one fundamental reason:

MEDDICC sees the qualification as a process that occurs throughout your deal's lifecycle. In contrast, most other frameworks see qualification as a one-time event or a stage that you have to pass.

An excellent example of the divide between MEDDICC and other frameworks can be found by comparing MEDDICC to BANT, which is the most popular qualification framework used by Sellers.

MEDDICC versus BANT

IBM developed BANT in the 1950s, and despite being over 60 years old, BANT is still widely used by Sellers, and for good reason. BANT quickly orientates the Seller onto four elements that will soon help to identify if the customer is qualified to buy.

BANT is based on the acronym of:

B - Budget: Does the customer have the budget available to them?

A - Authority: Does the customer have the authority to buy?

N - Need: Does the customer have enough need (pain) to buy?

T - Timing: Does the customer know when they are going to buy?

The fundamental difference between BANT and MEDDICC is that once you have satisfied the BANT elements, it is unusual for it to be referenced again in your deal. Whereas MEDDICC is a deal qualification methodology. It helps Sellers qualify if they should be in a deal at the start, but it also allows Sellers to continuously qualify, not just whether they should be in the deal but whether they are on top or behind.

While it is hard to argue against the concept that two sales qualification methodologies are similar, comparing BANT to MEDDICC is like comparing traveling to the shops on your bike to going to the moon in a rocket. Both take you from one place to another, but the level of detail is vastly different.

I do not mean to be derogatory of BANT. It is a highly useful framework to empower SDRs and Inside Sellers to obtain an early steer on an opportunity, but at Enterprise-level selling, it leaves a lot to be desired.

My favorite analogy is to imagine that if selling was a computer game, BANT would represent the EASY difficulty setting. In contrast, MEDDICC would be a more difficult setting, and when used correctly, it would be the highest difficulty setting where only Elite Sellers can play to its full potential.

Perhaps I should have renamed this book 'How to go from Amateur to Elite in the Game of Sales'.

Other Qualification Methodologies are Available

BANT isn't the only other qualification methodology. In recent years, there have been many new frameworks that come out with the promise to replace BANT. Unfortunately, for the reasons described earlier in this chapter and illustrated below, these frameworks still miss the mark as they serve qualification as if it is a binary state that, once passed, needs no further consideration.

Effectiveness at Stage

	Prospecting	Qualifying	Discovery	Demo	Proposal	Manage the Close	Handover
ANUM							
BANT							
CHAMP							
FAINT							
GPCTBA/C&I							
MEDDICC							

You can find my perspective on other Qualification Methodologies in the Appendix of this book.

BANT and MEDDICC are not Enemies

All of this said, BANT and MEDDICC are not enemies of each other. In fact, they can work together. Many hugely successful sales teams will use both BANT and MEDDICC in their sales processes with SDRs using BANT to obtain an initial qualification on deals they create before passing the deal over to a Seller.

The rationale for this is usually that BANT is more user-friendly for SDR's and MEDDICC is too complicated for the initial engagement, which is, of course, true if you approach it as assuming you need to answer every element of it. This misunderstanding represents why many qualification methodologies, including BANT and MEDDICC, get a bad name because junior salespeople feel they need to check off answers to every element during every engagement with a customer. Being on the other side of this process feels like an interrogation for the customer and is unlikely to achieve the desired results. Instead, Sellers should adapt their approach to allow for a conversation that focuses on uncovering the qualification elements, not just for their own needs but also for helping the customer understand theirs.

Nobody has ever described this better than Ron Willingham did in his book 'Integrity Selling for the 21st Century':

"The art of persuasion is a paradox. The more we attempt to persuade people, the more they tend to resist us. But the more we attempt to understand and create value for them, the more they tend to persuade themselves."

Or as Blair Warren says in his book, The Forbidden Keys to Persuasion:

"People rarely argue with their own conclusions."

Within the Discovery chapter of this book, we will discuss how to have sales conversations that uncover useful information for the Seller and help move the buyer's mindset into a position where you can help them better understand their goals, challenges, and pains.

QUALIFICATION

MEDDICC is a qualification methodology for enterprise sales. While by proxy, the majority of this book is about qualification, it is still an important enough element that it deserves its own chapter.

As a Seller in enterprise sales, you are likely to have a territory—whether geographic, vertical, or by named accounts. You most likely have a go-to-market team assisting you in finding leads and technical support in the form of a solution consultant or sales engineer. When you combine all of the resources you have at your disposal, it is almost like you have a franchise within the organization you work for, only you didn't have to buy it, and they pay you a salary. If you take this franchise mindset into qualification, you'll quickly realize that the only resource you truly have is time.

Time is a Sellers Most Precious Asset

Time is a Seller's most precious asset. Yet, Sellers are frivolous with their time, chasing after unqualified opportunities, or worse, opportunities that they have qualified but aren't a good fit.

This is a harsh lesson to learn, and I sometimes wonder whether I would ever have had the chance to fully embrace it if I hadn't led a sales team for an organization that's product-market fit was extremely narrow. A post-mortem on a poor Q3 made me realize that we had gone too broadly out of our narrow comfort zone. While the early metrics had looked great with lots of meetings being booked and pipeline being built, the conversion rates fell through the floor. If we had been better at qualifying earlier in the quarter, we would have been able to change course sooner and be proactive, not reactive.

It was clear that we needed to shift our focus for the fourth quarter to where we had product-market fit. As this was such a narrow lane, the number of meetings and pipeline shrank drastically, but the conversion rate went through the roof, from less than 5% in Q3 to over 30% in Q4. Better still, we went on to not only hit the quarterly number by doubling our best ever quarter, but we also hit the annual target, making up for the significant shortfall in Q3.

As crazy as it may sound, that experience wasn't enough to convince me of the importance of qualifying deals relentlessly as in the very next quarter. A senior leadership appointment had pushed the commercial organization back onto the course of going after the broader market. While I disagreed and presented a counter-strategy to expand into countries where we had a product-market fit, I should have been more resolute in my position. The next two quarters turned out to be the worst in the companies' history, despite doubling the sales team. It cost the new executive his job and the shareholders of the company a likely substantial drop in valuation.

The above is an example of poor qualification at the macro-level, but at the micro-level as an individual contributor, it hurts the Sellers. In the previous quarter, a new Seller did over 60% of his annual target in the fourth quarter alone and didn't sell a single thing for the following two quarters.

I am sure you have your own scars from when you should have qualified out of a deal but didn't.

The Qualification Equation

If there is one thing I guarantee will make you a more successful Seller, it is improving your ability to qualify. The equation is simple: by qualifying better, you will either save time by removing effort on deals that you are unlikely to win or uncover data points that can help you succeed.

However, Sellers often opt to use the flawed and disproven: effort + time = success equation, which is a slippery slope and often leads to the Fallacy of Sunken Costs.

The Fallacy of Sunken Costs

By the time the first call with a customer comes around, you and your team may have invested hours into the opportunity. From initial research, stakeholder mapping, and perhaps a demand generation element, to anything from webinars, events, or sales development work. It is easy to get carried away and lost in the classic Fallacy of the Sunken Cost. This is where you ignore the telltale signs that the deal isn't going to qualify, but because you have invested so much effort, you persist and try and work the deal into a qualified state, or perhaps just ignore the Risks and proceed forward, squinting your eyes shut to the obvious while crossing your fingers behind your back and telling your manager "there's a deal to be done here."

It is essential to specify that there is a difference between having a first call where you identify that the opportunity doesn't qualify and one where you have been unable to qualify. The latter scenario most likely means you have more discovery to do, but the former will say that you have uncovered information to inform you that the opportunity isn't qualified. This could be due to several reasons, but the most common are:

No Pain/Willingness to Change

If you haven't been able to uncover enough pain or a willingness to change the pain you have discovered, then this is a pretty strong signal that you should qualify out. An exception may be where you feel these circumstances may be limited to the person or department you are talking to, and via working with other stakeholders, you may find more pain/willingness to change.

Your Solution Doesn't Fit

A common qualification error is when Sellers identify that their solution doesn't fit the solution's requirements or may solve some elements of the requirement. Still, it isn't a good fit, and yet they persevere with the opportunity trying to make their square peg solution fit through the customer's round hole problem.

Usually, this is because the Seller can't stand to lose, or they are perhaps just happy to have a customer that wants to talk to them. Either way, if they don't drastically change the solution's scope, then qualifying out is the only option.

Your Contacts Have No Influence

If the contacts you are talking to don't have the influence to get a deal done or to introduce you to a stakeholder who does have influence, then you should qualify out and treat the customer as a new prospect. It may be useful to use the call as a discovery session to help you uncover pains and alternative stakeholders. Still, without a warm introduction, this opportunity is at a dead-end, emphasizing the word 'dead.'

If the Customer Refuses to Allow You to do Discovery

Much rarer is the inexperienced buyer who refuses the Seller the opportunity to do any kind of discovery. Their favorite phrase is, "We are not here to tell you about us, we are here for you to tell us about your solution." Of course, Sellers should politely push back and try to persevere with discovery, but if the customer remains uncooperative, you should qualify out of the opportunity. I have never met a customer who does this and has enough seniority to get a deal done, and I doubt you will either. Regardless, without being able to do discovery, you are selling blind and most likely wasting your time.

If You are in Doubt, Qualify Out

It is my firm belief that if you have any concerns about the qualification of your deal after applying MEDDICC to it, you should qualify out.

Qualifying out because of doubt will commonly have one of two effects:

1. Your customer will accept your position and rationale for not pursuing the opportunity with them further.

2. Your customer will disagree with your position and try to convince you why you should pursue the opportunity with them.

Win/Win.

Effect one will allow you to move onto a better-qualified opportunity. Effect two will allow you to pivot and go more in-depth on the qualification with your customer to better qualify them.

> *"I regret qualifying out of that opportunity."*
> *- Nobody ever.*

The next chapter talks about the attributes that define an elite Seller of which qualification is one, but, in particular, having the foresight to be able to qualify out is at the epitome of elite selling.

How you qualify your deal will evolve as you move through the sales process, with each stage bringing different considerations. Let's take a closer look at the qualification and the sales process.

Qualifying in the Sales Process

No matter where you are in the sales process, you can check your deal against MEDDICC to obtain a quick qualification check and spot areas that need closer investigation. Where you are in your sales process will dictate the things in particular that you should look for.

Qualifying in the Early-Stages

Potentially, the easiest place to qualify a deal is within the early stages. However, it is also where most mistakes are made as Sellers either choose to ignore the red flags or feel as though they can power through them by pitching harder.

Parts of MEDDICC to Analyze Carefully in the Early-Stages:

Metrics and Implicate the Pain - Have you found enough pain that when it is quantified, it makes a compelling case for an evaluation of your solution?

Champion and Economic Buyer - Do you have a good understanding of who your Champion is or is likely to be? Do you have a good understanding of the stakeholders and who the Economic Buyer is?

If you can't answer the above questions affirmatively, it doesn't mean you should qualify out; it means you should be prioritizing getting affirmative responses. If you are unable to, it is then that you should qualify out.

Qualifying in the Mid-Stages

By this stage, you should have qualified that there is pain and who the Champion and the Economic Buyer is. Your focus should now shift towards qualifying the Decision and Competition elements of the deal and going more in-depth on the Metrics and Pain.

Parts of MEDDICC to Analyze Carefully in the Mid-Stages:

Metrics and Implicate the Pain - Have you been building robust Metrics that portray the value in which your solution will be measured? Do you have a consensus with the customer?

Decision Criteria and Decision Process - Do you have a full understanding of the Criteria in which the customer will decide and the process they will undergo to come to that decision?

Champion and Economic Buyer - Have you tested your Champion? Do they have power and influence? Are they actively selling internally for you? Do they have a personal win? Have you engaged directly with the Economic Buyer? Are they aware of the Metrics?

Competition - Do you have sight of who your Competition is? Have you been able to lay effective traps for them? Do you have a plan in place to counter?

Qualifying Out in the Late-Stages

If you have deployed it correctly, MEDDICC should act as a map in the late stages of the deal that clearly shows you exactly where you are in your deal, where you have left to go, and any uncovered territory.

At the Late Stages, you should be focused on ensuring your Metrics are fully understood and embraced by the customer, particularly with the Economic Buyer. You will want to have consensus with your Champion as to where you are in the Decision and Paper Processes.

Parts of MEDDICC to Analyze Carefully in the Late-Stages

Metrics and Implicate the Pain - You should have the Metrics locked in with consensus from the key stakeholders. The pain should be fully quantified and implicated upon the customer.

Economic Buyer - You should have good engagement and a consensus with the Economic Buyer on the Metrics.

Decision Criteria - You should have a full understanding of the Decision Criteria and how you score against it.

Decision Process - You should fully understand the Decision Process and where you are within it.

Paper Process - You should have a full understanding of the Paper Process and where you are against it.

If you have used MEDDICC, it is far less likely that you will find yourself qualifying out at the late stages, but it can happen, and the Sunken Cost Fallacy, as described earlier in this chapter, plays an even more significant role by the time we get to the late stages. After all, you've come this far, what have you got to lose, right? **Everything!**

In enterprise sales, the stakes are usually at their highest when your deal is in the late stages. Not only will this represent a significant investment of time and resources from you and your team, but it is also likely that you are forecasting the deal to some degree. Just like with forecast accuracy—the most defining factor of a Seller's ability—you do not want to get it wrong at this stage.

By the late stages, you should have earned the right to ask all of the difficult questions to ensure you are correctly forecasting your deal.

Don't Be Afraid to Qualify

Sellers sometimes act like ostriches and stick their heads in the sand to avoid late-stage qualification, hoping that any Risk that has been highlighted will fade away if they just ignore it.

You should approach any uncovered Risk head-on. The only reason Sellers avoid doing this is because they are afraid of upsetting their customer or the deal, but if the Risk isn't dealt with, it will derail your deal anyway.

Being brave and bold will help you win, not lose. The case study below gives a real-world example of where this was true:

Qualifying to win with MEDDICC - Being Bold, Differentiating, and Covering Competition

Working for: Enterprise Provider of Social Media SaaS

Selling to: Global Media Company and Producer of Hit TV-Shows

We were invited by a global media organization headquartered in Amsterdam to pitch to become their social media management solution. We knew early on that while it wasn't going to be an RFP process, it would be a thorough evaluation. We knew this as we were able to uncover within the first call that they were evaluating us based on our inclusion in a Forrester Leaders Wave. With this information, we were able to confirm who our Competition was and what the Decision Criteria and Process were (I love the Dutch, they are so straight-up about everything!).

Risks Galore

We identified two early Risks that we knew we had to get a hold of quickly:

The first was that the Forrester report referred to was led by an analyst who favored our main rival. While we came out in a similar position in the overall report, this analyst was no friend of ours. The organization we were selling to had mentioned that speaking to him was part of their Decision Process.

The second Risk was that the customer's organization was owned by another organization that happened to be our rival's number one reference customer in Europe. Our Dutch friends let us know this early on and notified us that they could procure licenses for the rival's software through the group, saving time and hassle. Ouch!

These Risks were not to be taken lightly. My manager at the time told me to qualify out, and it was only because I protested and said that I think we had a unique differentiator that he let me pursue the opportunity, stating that I could use it to 'practice my pitch' as I was relatively new at the time. However, he mandated that we weren't allowed to travel to meet the customer, which added another Risk that we were seen to not be as heavily invested in winning the customer's business.

Finding a Differentiator

There was only one way we stood a chance of winning this deal, and that was to find a unique differentiator. We knew we had one early on, which was that our solution had a rules engine built into it, meaning that you could create workflows based on the classic 'if this then that' ruleset. This was a strong differentiator for us in so many engagements because, as social media software, it was essential to send inbound messages to the right places. An example of this would be how a major CPG brand would want to triage messages that may mention a word like 'poison' with urgency. But, what about a broadcaster? After a brainstorming session, we had a breakthrough idea; the organization created live TV talent shows and much of what they wanted social media software for was to better manage their engagement with their audience during the live broadcasts, but trying to filter through the firehose of engagement would have been an impossible task without some kind of automation. All hail the rules engine!

So, we had a unique differentiator. The task was now to Implicate the Pain related to it and apply Metrics that the customer would agree to. Once we had this, then we could work on trying to get it into the Decision Criteria.

Implicating the Pain of Life Without our Differentiator

The process of Implicating the Pain relating to this differentiator followed a classic 'Three I's' transition where we first Identified the Pain to the customer by asking questions about what plans they had to manage the inflow of engagement on social media while live shows were on. Their answer was that they would have teams of people set up to handle the inbound engagement throughout the shows. We quickly discovered this was going to be a mix of people from various existing teams and some new teams they had to create.

We had Identified the Pain that our unique differentiator could help solve as our rules engine could help automate the inbound engagement and prioritize it based on the criteria that the customer configured. For example, if a celebrity or person with similar social influence Tweeted about the show, we could put that into a priority queue for immediate attention.

We were armed with the information we needed to Indicate the Pain to the customer. To do this, we required more information about the volume of inbound messages and had to make some estimations about the salary costs of those who would be hired to manage engagement during the live shows. Another angle we considered was, what would the perceived cost be of missing a high-value interaction? We asked, "What if Justin Bieber Tweets at you, and you miss it?" We didn't ask this question to uncover lost revenue; instead, we wanted to ask the customer to make them consider those circumstances, the missed opportunity, and the repercussions of them. By causing the customer to consider this negative scenario, we were forcing them to feel Implicated by the pain, which is the final step of the Three I's transition: Identify pain> Indicate pain> Implicate pain.

This was an example of a thorough two-sided discovery process, of which you can learn more about in the upcoming Discovery chapter. The key takeaway from this part is to recollect how important it was that we identified a differentiator and that we were able to Indicate the pain it causes and to Implicate that pain for the customer.

Adding to the Decision Criteria

Once we had Indicated how significant the pain was to the customer, and they felt Implicated enough to solve it, we had to get the pain added to the Decision Criteria.

As you will learn within the Decision Criteria Chapter, this isn't always a straightforward process, mostly because your customers won't necessarily have a black and white Decision Criteria that they are referring to. It will often fall under a specification, a requirements document, or just a consensus among the stakeholders of 'stuff' they need.

In this instance, the most influential stakeholders in the engagement were the technical decision-makers, whose interest was primarily around technical validation of our solution and were less interested in the criteria outside of this. This was bad news for our Automation use case as it was seen from a technical perspective as 'nice to have'.

To get around this challenge, we had to work with our Champion to re-engage the marketing stakeholder, who we learned had given his blessing for the procurement of either our solution or our rivals'. His re-engagement was a game-changer for us as his reaction to the automation use-case was spectacular. On the call we were on, he called out just how much of a headache it would solve. Of course, we dug deeper to get him to talk about the strain that having to hire people to manage the social engagement would cost him. He obliged in our Implication of his pain perfectly as the call turned into what felt more like a counseling session for what his woes would be without our solution. Perfect!

The puzzle's final piece was to discuss the requirement with my Champion, who agreed that it had become an important consideration for them. This was as far as I pushed it. Whether or not you want to push further on a matter like this comes down to your style and personality as a Seller. In this case, I played a little naive and rather than going down the somewhat obvious route of calling out our rival not having the rules engine, I questioned:

> *"Do you think this is an essential enough requirement that the solution you select will need to have it?"*

> *"Will, the discovery of solutions that have automation that could save thousands of Euros in salaries mean you can obtain a higher budget to pay for it?"*

You may notice that both of these questions are close-ended. While nine out of ten discovery questions you ask should be open-ended, in this case, I wanted my Champion to bluntly answer for their benefit as much as for my own.

He answered that he felt it would be important, but they didn't confirm that it was a must-have requirement. I assumed this was because they knew it was unique to my solution. Even though this person was my Champion, his first loyalty was to his company, where keeping a competitive process was within their interest. He also said there wouldn't be any extra budget. This was an expected response.

The Champion Bluff

Our Champion gave us the nod that we were unofficially their preferred partner. A statement wrapped with all kinds of cave-ats—mainly the Risks we had called out early on, such as the threat from the group already having a relationship with our rival and the Forrester analyst who had been engaged directly to the customer by our rival. The final part of the Decision Process was to obtain a commercial agreement.

This was not going to be an easy feat. We were considerably higher in cost than our rival, but our rival was also operating from the position of a pre-negotiated group deal. It took any pricing gamesmanship off the table for them and created an even more significant divide between our pricing and theirs. Our price was seven times that of our rival's, who had also included unlimited user licenses and volumes. It was a genuine all you could eat scenario, whereas our proposition was limited on both fronts.

This negotiation remains one of my favorites, mostly because of the Economic Buyer's brilliance, who, in this case, was the CTO. In a strategy straight out of the top shelf of the negotiating master's playbook, he pretended not to speak English. I don't know whether you have ever tried to negotiate with anyone via a translator before, but it is really hard! In the Seller's seat, you feel like your negotiation points have no grounds, and every point your customer makes goes unanswered.

We left the negotiation in a bit of a stalemate. The customer wasn't going to pay 7x more for our solution and their primary negotiation stance was that the CTO would take the 'Risk' in going against the group's recommendation of our rival, but he wouldn't do so if it cost more. I had almost learned Dutch for "I would lose my job over this", I had heard it so much in the negotiation.

Before we could make any advances in the negotiation, we needed to get past the customer's sticking point of stating they wouldn't pay more than our rival's price, meaning that we would need an 86% discount to get to their price, which was wholly untenable.

It all came to a head in a call with my Champion, where he was reasserting their position that they wouldn't pay anywhere near our cost. I very bluntly pointed out that while our price was 7x our rival's, the data between the two amounts was nothing compared to the additional expenses their business would have without the business processes the rules engine would allow them to streamline, and that if they were unable to see that additional value comes with the additional cost, then perhaps we weren't the right partners for them and we should adjourn our engagement.

At this moment, I had made my peace with the situation. We had done everything right, and if that wasn't enough, then it would be a shame, but I knew the team had executed everything perfectly.

This was indeed an example of where we were qualifying out at one of the latest stages possible.

Except, we weren't! My Champion responded, stating words that have stuck with me ever since:

> *"No, we don't have to do that; we just need to find the price that works for both of us."*

BINGO! The glimmer of light we needed. They were prepared to pay more for our solution. It took us threatening to walk away for them to show their hand.

In the end, we lowered some of the scopes and made some concessions to get to just over the 3x cost of our rival. Within six months, the customer expanded their use of our solution, putting their contract value far above the 7x figure initially quoted. They went on to become a massive supporter of ours in Europe, completing numerous case studies and reference calls for us.

All of that said, my two favorite facts about this deal were:

1. That I later learned that the CTO spoke excellent English, there is even a video of him talking on stage at a major event. He pretended not to speak English as a negotiation tactic. Brilliant!

2. I went on to sell to my Champion again at another company I worked for, proving that, with a true Champion, you can have disagreements and still work through them. To this day, we are friends on social networks and keep in contact.

Throughout the engagement with this customer, MEDDICC played a critical role. Without it, there is no shadow of a doubt in my mind that we would have not only lost the deal, but we would have been unable to identify the aspects that would have helped us to win. Instead, we would have spent just as much time in the deal without a chance of winning.

WHAT DEFINES ELITE?

The shortest answer I can give to this question is simply:

" Forecast Accuracy."

Sure, not all accurate forecasters are Elite Sellers, but all Elite Sellers are accurate forecasters.

To be elite, you need to have a particular set of attributes that we will cover in this chapter. Among those attributes, you have to be efficient. More specifically, to be elite, you have to be a relentless qualifier.

Relentless Qualifiers

Elite Sellers value their time, and therefore, they relentlessly qualify their deals to make sure they are worth their time.

Having a focus on efficiency will increase your productivity because you will be focusing your time on good deals. It also means you exude an air of confidence that your customers will recognize as you valuing your time, perhaps because you have so many customers queuing up to do business with you.

Learning this is one of the hardest things for Sellers to grasp. Some never do. We all know that Seller who chases after every opportunity like an over-excited Dalmatian pup chases after a stick, then a duck, then a stick, then whatever looks shiny next.

MEDDICC forces Sellers to ask themselves the hard qualification questions about their deals. Even the most unfocused, 'happy eared' Sellers will find it hard to argue with MEDDICC's conclusions about their deals.

Sales is Performance-Based

Selling is a performance-based profession just like a sport, and like any sport, some factors consistently lead to success in Sellers just as they do in athletes. I have been fascinated by this concept for a long time. It could probably be the subject of an entire book on its own, but I have distilled it down into five categories of performance-related attributes:

1. Intelligence
2. Hard Working
3. Always Learning
4. Practice and Preparation
5. Process

Let's go a little deeper on each one:

1. Intelligence

This one is undeniably a part of any Seller's success. Many factors equate to intelligence in Sellers, but it predominantly comes down to ICE:

1. IQ
2. Curiosity
3. EQ (Emotional Intelligence)

Being naturally high in intelligence is fundamental to a Seller's success rate as intelligence will not only help Sellers to establish and understand the circumstances they find themselves in quickly, but they will also hold high credibility with their customers as they are more likely to be seen as a trustworthy authority on solving their pains.

Sellers can improve all three ICE attributes. You can enhance your perceived IQ by learning more about business, your industry, and your solution. Focusing on trying to be more curious will give the impression of having a higher EQ.

A critical component of being curious is listening, which also relates to how your EQ will be perceived.

2. Hard Working

I used to play football for my local team and in the locker room was a sign across the back wall that said:

Hard work beats talent when talent doesn't work hard.

I loved that quote. It was especially true for me as I was never the most talented footballer; I would say that the only reason I held my place in the teams I played for was how hardworking I was.

I could say the same for my sales career after building a successful early career in selling software solutions to SME's where I got my lucky break with an interview for an up and coming software company called Kontagent. Ahead of the interview, I devoured every single piece of data I could find on them. I genuinely think I knew more about the company than the newly appointed sales leader who was interviewing me. Unfortunately, I never got past the first interview. This wasn't some grand injustice; I didn't yet have the experience for the role. However, as part of my obsessive research-level ahead of the interview, I reached out to a Seller in the US to ask for interview advice. He replied after I had my interview with a very blunt:

"I wouldn't bother. We only seem to hire people from Oracle."

"Oracle?!" I thought. I assumed Oracle only made databases at the time. However, after further exploration, I learned that they had an up and coming SaaS business, and I reached out to a recruiter thinking to myself:

"if I want the cool job like Kontagent, I've got to do my time at Oracle."

My timing couldn't have been better; Oracle was on a mission to grow its SaaS business, and I was invited to an 'Assessment Day,' which can only be described as 'The Apprentice'. It was a day-long event where over 80 candidates were assessed for a role in Oracle. Again, my work ethic helped me prevail as I felt I scored particularly well on the presentations where I was able to prepare well.

The final stage with Oracle was an interview with the VP of Sales, accompanied by two people from the recruitment team and my hiring manager.

In the session, the VP highlighted the relevant education gaps in my resume; specifically that there weren't any qualifications (I am a high school dropout). The VP said:

> *"Oracle is a learning company, and I need to be able to see some proof that you can learn."*

Fortunately, I had self-taught myself to build websites and demonstrate some live sites that quickly rectified the VP's concern. However, after all of that, after a whole week of preparation and a day filled with various exercises and tests, I almost blew it by not closing the VP at the end of the interview:

VP: "OK, I think I have asked you all I need to know. Do you have any questions for me?"

Me: "Um no, thank you. I think you have answered all the questions I have."

VP: "Are you sure there isn't a question you would like to ask me before we finish?"

Me: "Err," *vigorously looks at notes*, "well err, what is your biggest challen—"

VP: *cuts me off* "No. I am not going to answer that.... There is a question you must want to ask me."

Me: "OH! Right, yes... OK, are there any concerns you have seen from our conversation or the sessions today that make you feel like I wouldn't be able to fulfill the role here at Oracle?"

VP: "Right, thank you. *Gets up and leaves.*

I got the job at Oracle, but I was vastly out of my depth. My role was to sell Enterprise Resource Planning (ERP) software to the most prominent organizations in the UK. It was one of the most complex sales with some of the most complex customers.

I was never going to hit my ERP target, but I worked hard and found a single opportunity to show my potential to other business units. A manager asked me to transfer to his team where I could find some success selling marketing solutions that were much easier to understand. I found success, and the same headhunter that had approached me for the Kontagent role just over two years earlier got in touch about a position at a company called Sprinklr.

Sprinklr was everything I loved about Kontagent and more. I had always been interested in the social media space, and Sprinklr had a much stronger proposition and a brighter future. I took the same level of preparation into the interviews with Sprinklr as I did Kontagent and Oracle and got the job.

Sprinklr was where I first learned MEDDICC, and their investment in me set me on the path of success I have been on and, ultimately, led me to write this book.

The moral of this story is a simple one – hard work. Without the hard work going into the Kontagent role, I'd never have found out that startups like Kontagent and Sprinklr like to hire people from Oracle, and I'd never have gone to do my 'time' there, nor would I have gotten the job at Oracle without hard work. After all, there was very little evidence that I had the intelligence for those roles at the time.

3. Always Learning

Elite Sellers know that selling is a science and an art. No scientist or artist ever stops learning, and neither will a Seller.

In his book *How Rich People Think*, Steve Siebold interviewed 1,200 of the world's wealthiest people on their habits. One commonality was that they were all relentless readers.

No matter where you look, you will find a correlation between increasing knowledge and success, and you don't just have to read. Thanks to the internet, Sellers can now learn from audiobooks, podcasts, Ted Talks, YouTube, Masterclass, and hundreds of other resources.

Often, Sellers will be within teams with other Sellers, and if the teams are well organized, there are likely to be sessions such as deal reviews where Sellers can drop in to learn from their peers' experiences.

Today, there are even technology platforms that automatically record customer calls, pick out keywords, and sentiment from the conversation. Elite Sellers can review their calls to spot areas for improvement. They can ask their peers for feedback on the sessions and listen to their colleagues' calls to learn from their interactions.

4. Practice and Preparation

Elite Sellers, just like elite athletes, spend hours practicing. Before a tournament, an elite tennis player will practice their serve over and over. They wouldn't turn up to a match and start practicing with their opponent. But, Sellers do this all of the time:

Sellers spend hours researching their customers, doing discovery, and subsequently compiling the information into a proposition that they can present without practicing it or getting feedback from their peers.

"We practice our presentations on our customers."

Sellers sometimes spend months working on a deal. They get to a crunch point where they are having a critical conversation with a department like Procurement, and they roll up without having prepared for – or practiced – what may happen. The result is that they get eaten alive by Procurement who have conversations with Sellers every day.

> *"We practice our negotiations on our customers."*

Think of the last time a customer raised an objection with you. The chances are you did an OK job of answering it, but imagine if you could pause and rewind time to answer it again. I bet the second time of explaining it, you would be more convincing and articulate. This is precisely what you should practice for.

You can and should practice on your own. For a presentation, in the book The Art of The Start by Guy Kawasaki, he states that a business pitch only begins to sound truly solid after 25 deliveries. If it is a presentation of your solution, you may not need to go into such depth, but there should be an amount of personalization within the presentation that requires practice.

For other engagements that aren't presentations, you should prepare. Ahead of every sales engagement, ask yourself questions like:

- What outcome do I want from this engagement?
- Who else do I want to speak to?
- Have I set the expectation ahead of time? Agenda, etc.?
- What objections could be raised?
- What messages do I need to reinforce?

5. Process

Without exception, every single elite Seller I have ever known is process-driven. Elite Sellers understand that sales is a science as much as an art. The most effective way to succeed is to follow the anatomy of success, which should correlate to how your organization has structured its sales process.

By contrast, the worst Sellers I know aren't process-driven. Their definition of following a process starts and stops with updating the deal stage within their CRM system.

Be a Plotter not a Pantser

I recently learned two terms that writers have to describe novelists:

Plotters and Pantsers.

Plotters plan out their novel before they write it, whereas Pantsers fly by the seat of their pants; pretty much meaning they make it up as they go along.

While Stephen King and George R. R. Martin write fantastic fiction novels by being Pantsers, I'm sure you'll agree that there is little room for fiction in your forecast.

Elite Sellers are plotters.

Qualifying Out

As mentioned at the beginning of this chapter, Elite Sellers are relentless qualifiers. They know that the best way to protect their time is by qualifying out of opportunities that don't meet their qualification standards.

I once knew a sales leader who wanted a deal stage to be added to their CRM called 'Closed Lost with Hope.' Deals on this stage would be omitted from the forecast, but would still be worked on by Sellers in the (desperate) hope they come back to life. I think this is a terrible idea; if you are a Seller and find yourself in the emergency room doing CPR on your deals, there is something very wrong with your qualification process.

When you start relentlessly qualifying your deals and subsequently qualifying out of those you deem as unqualified, you will notice two surprising by-products:

1. Customers will increase their interest and self-qualify themselves. Sometimes inexperienced buyers pretend

they are less interested than they are, and by calling their bluff, you'll force them to show their hand.

2. Those where you have correctly qualified out will often come back to you when they are ready. If you hadn't qualified, you might have pursued this organization incorrectly and burnt up sales capital to get them to commit when they weren't qualified to do so.

Summary

In summary, each attribute listed in this chapter can help a Seller towards being good. However, as per the following examples, without having all five of the elite attributes, it is highly unlikely you will be defined as elite:

If you lack intelligence, you are likely to miss cues that your customer is giving you. You will be less articulate and slower to handle objections. If you have a low EQ, it is likely to make dealing with you a terrible experience for your customer.

If you lack the drive to be hardworking, it will mean you continuously miss opportunities to make progress, and your competition will always beat you with a better work ethic.

If you lack the will to learn, it will leave you falling over the same mistakes time and time again. Moreover, you Risk being left behind as the industry moves forward with innovations that you won't understand.

If you lack the ability to practice and prepare, then you will never be at your best. Appearing unprepared to your customer will kill any credibility that you have obtained by having strength in the other attributes.

If you lack the process, then every time you win, you'll feel that you got lucky or your talent won you the deal. This may seem OK until you realize that, by contrast, you are never going to know why you lost, except for that you were 'unlucky' or the customer was stupid.

DISCOVERY

Discovery is the most critical part of any enterprise sale. No other element will have such a significant impact on the success of your deal.

When executed correctly, discovery is the primary technique used to extract information that converts into value for the customer. It is also the leading technique Sellers use to qualify whether they should be pursuing an opportunity with the customer.

Discovery is the technique that ties the MEDDICC methodology to the information within the customer's business. Without discovery, MEDDICC simply cannot be effective.

Further still, a fantastic by-product of discovery is that by approaching your customer in a thoughtful and well-researched manner, you can demonstrate at the earliest opportunity that you have a credible point of view that may open up their mind to knowledge and challenges they have not yet considered.

Discovery is not a Stage

Despite what many organizations or the top 20 results on Google would have you believe, discovery is not something that starts and finishes on your first call, nor is it a stage in your sales process.

Discovery is a mindset.

Always Be Curious

The legendary scene from the movie Glengarry Glen Ross with Alec Baldwin scathing a team of real estate agents where he says the infamous line "ABC – Always Be Closing" should be flipped in enterprise sales to "Always Be Curious."

In enterprise sales, you always have to be curious because deals are alive, fluid, and continually changing. New Decision Criteria gets added all of the time, the Decision Process shifts, new stakeholders become involved and old ones disengage or leave the company. An average enterprise sales cycle can last months, and if you limit yourself to doing discovery on a first call, then from that point on, you will always be selling with historical information.

Being Curious means Actively Listening

> "Listen with curiosity. Speak with honesty. Act with integrity. The greatest problem with communication is that we don't listen to understand. We listen to reply. When we listen with curiosity, we don't listen with the intent to reply. We listen for what's behind the words."
> - Roy T. Bennett, The Light in the Heart

The above quote from Roy T. Bennett epitomizes the difference between how an emotionally intelligent Seller approaches discovery compared to one with a lower EQ.

What Roy T. Bennett is referring to is what is widely known as 'Active Listening', which is where you make a conscious effort to hear not only the words that are being said but, crucially, the message that is being communicated within the words.

To actively listen in your discovery process, you need to:

- Truly listen to what your customer is saying. Don't just be looking for angles to sell against.

- Play back what you have heard. Whether you paraphrase or use your own words depends on your style and the situation.

- Get a confirmation that you understood by asking, "Have I understood that correctly?" This won't only ensure you have understood but it shows you care that you do.

- Go deeper by using two-sided discovery and open-ended questions, as explained later in this chapter.

By Actively Listening, you will be demonstrating that you care and as Theodore Roosevelt once said:

> *"No one cares how much you know until they know how much you care."*
> *- Theodore Roosevelt*

When the customer feels that you care and value their thoughts, they are more likely to elaborate upon them, thus opening the conversation to more in-depth discovery.

Mirror
&
Label

All of this will help you build an understanding with your customer: the nucleus of your relationship and the trust that needs to be made between you both.

When you do all of this well, you will build trust with your customer based upon the credibility you have made by showing the integrity that you aren't just hunting for things to sell against, but rather that you genuinely care about their business. This will allow you to ask the big questions that will set you up to uncover the most valuable information.

The Big Questions:

There are seven types of big questions that are super starting points for uncovering valuable information early in your deal cycle. They can come in many forms, but they generally sound like:

1. What is working?
2. What is not working?
3. When it works, what good things happen?
4. When it does not work, what bad things happen?
5. Whom does that affect?

6. How much does that cost?

7. Why haven't you tried to solve it yet?

The 7 big questions aren't necessarily the questions you ask. They represent the intention of your question. For example, you may not specifically ask:

"What is working?"

Instead, you'll ask something like:

"I read in your annual report that digital sales have grown 40% this year, what do you attribute your success to?"

As you can imagine, that question is likely to open up an interesting discussion about their growth. Once you feel you have uncovered enough positive information from this track, you can switch to a question like:

"Even though 40% is impressive, is there anything that you think held you back from growing even more?"

Quantify the Value

Whenever possible, you should be quantifying value against the information you uncover. Following on from the example question above, if we had learned that not having local language support in the Chinese market had held back the growth, we could ask:

"How much additional growth do you think you would have got if you had Chinese language support and were able to sell to China?

If the customer responded with a percentage, we could then ask:

*"How much incremental revenue do you think that X%
would have given you?"*

From this process, we have both quantified the value of adding Chinese Language support and having a figure to work with that represents the correlation between their digital growth and incremental revenue.

Discovery is not a Race

Average Sellers are so often excited to start talking about their company and products that they race through discovery as quickly as they can.

These Sellers approach their customers with a bank of questions intended to uncover pains that they can then sell against. This experience is awful for the customer; they sit there while the Seller bluntly digs for pain that they know will be used against them to try and make them buy the Seller's solution.

This approach has a meager success rate. Not only will it frustrate your customer, causing them to be less likely to share any useful information, it also skips right over your earliest opportunity to build trust.

Earning Credibility

To earn credibility with customers at the early stages of a sales cycle, Sellers need to show that they've earned the right to engage with them. This part of the process starts with demonstrating your value to the customer as early as possible. This part of the process begins with research.

Research First

Before any call or meeting, the Seller should thoroughly research the customer's organization. This can be broken down into several categories:

The Organization:

What is the state of their business? Are they growing? Expanding? Making Acquisitions? Or are they in trouble? Under threat from competition? Here are a few super places to research:

- **The Annual Report** - For me, there is no better source of information than the annual report. Of course, it will be biased towards a positive outlook, but it should help you uncover what the strategic plans are and the overall state of the business.

- **Their Existing Tech Stack** - If you are selling a technical solution such as software, you can find a lot of useful information by analyzing what technology they already use. Plugins for your web browser, such as BuiltWith, will allow you to see what technology is running on a website. It will often state when the technology was implemented or when the website stopped using it.

- **News Articles and Press Releases** - Not only will the latest news and press keep you up to date with any current matters within the organization, but they also give clues to the organization's strategic direction.

Researching these sources doesn't just prime you with the knowledge; it also stops you from frustrating your customer by asking them questions that you could have gotten answers from elsewhere.

The Industry

Many Sellers have specializations in industries, so there may not be a specific requirement to research the sector ahead of a new engagement. However, if it is a new industry to you as a Seller, it is vital that you research the industry.

Understanding how the sector works, what trends are occurring, and understanding industry-specific terms will be necessary, especially if your organization is new to the industry or doesn't have many customers you can reference. If you are new to an industry, your competitors are likely to lay traps around your industry experience.

Look out for any significant industry changes that have occurred recently or are upcoming. These can be anything from acquisitions or mergers through to changes to the law that may affect the customer you are talking to.

The People

Start first with whom you are going to be engaging with.

- What is their role?
- What is likely to be their goals and challenges right now?
- Who are your mutual connections?
- Can anyone give you some advice or insight into dealing with this person? Where have they worked before?
- Would they have used your solution before or that of your competitors?
- What publicly available information can you find out about this person online? *I know of several instances where before meetings, Sellers have been researching a person they are going to meet only to find a video of them talking about their role and aims.*

There is an ethical line that shouldn't be overstepped. However, if for instance, the person has linked their Twitter account to their LinkedIn profile, then you should check out their Twitter feed to see if it gives any glimpse into their professional views or any publicly available information that may help you build rapport with them, such as supporting a charity, or that they are a keen cyclist, etc.

Use LinkedIn to gather an assumed org chart of people whom you think will be stakeholders within your deal, whom they may report to, and what their role may be within your deal. Having this information ready will help you quickly relate the information you hear in discovery to people and departments.

With your assumed org chart, try to research what each role does and what it is responsible for. Job titles rarely mean the same thing from one organization to another, so it is dangerous to assume someone's responsibilities. A proven hack for understanding more about stakeholders, their departments, and their duties is to look at the organization's job listings for both past and present roles. This will not only give you an insight into what departments are expanding or currently under change, but it will provide you with insight into the responsibilities of various roles.

Internal Parties

I am frequently surprised at just how often Sellers will engage in a new opportunity without taking advantage of the rich data that exists within their systems and teams. If you work in enterprise sales for a well-established company, your engagement with a customer is unlikely to be the first that your company has had. Therefore, it is likely that there are some valuable nuggets of information within your company, your colleagues' memories, or even your CRM system.

Third Parties

Whom do you know that understands your customer's business or the people that work there? By following all of the above advice, you are likely to uncover third parties who already have relationships. What can they tell you about them? This is particularly useful if they have recently been through a deal process with the organization. They can tell you what to expect and may know lots of helpful information relating to how they form their Decision Criteria, Decision, and Paper Processes as well as stakeholder information. Although, of course, caution should always be taken as it is likely that all of these things could be different for your deal.

One of my most successful encounters with third parties was when I was invited to an RFP with a company where I had no previous engagements. I knew three different Sellers who had sold to this company, so I took them all out for dinner.

As the drink flowed, so did the egos with each Seller trying to outdo the other by showing off their organization's expertise. By the end of the evening, I had four pages of notes and an incredible understanding of the company. I won the deal, and while I may have won without that dinner taking place, without any doubt, it contributed majorly towards shortening the timeframe and helping me focus on the right things.

Solution Base

Depending on the solution you sell, you may be able to make some assumptions about the organization by looking from the outside in. An example of this would be if you were selling a solution like Bazaarvoice, which enables reviews and ratings on e-commerce sites. As a Seller for Bazaarvoice, you will see whether the organization you are about to engage with has any reviews and rating software on their website. If they do, you will know who the incumbent is, and you are likely to have some assumptions about where they are feeling pain and areas your solution can provide value.

Remember, while the information you obtain from following the advice in this section is valuable, much of it will lead you to assumptions that are not factual. As the saying goes, "If you assume, you make an 'ass' out of 'u' and 'me'." You should highlight the assumptions you have made and seek clarity on them on the first call.

The First Call

Once you have completed your research, it is time to prepare for the first call. The first call isn't always a call, it can be a meeting, but oftentimes first meetings have multiple stakeholders within them and/or an expectation that you will present something in the meeting. So, therefore, it's good practice to set up the first call ahead of the first meeting to do discovery and validate your research.

Preparation is key

By this point, if you have followed the advice earlier in this chapter, you will have built up a robust picture of the state of the organization and an assumption of where you can add value. It is useful to consolidate and prepare this information in your first call.

I am a little old school when it comes to note-taking, and I love a notebook, but I've found the benefit of having a document I can share and collaborate on. It definitely trumps hand-written notes.

Your company may already have a place they want you to capture this information, whether it be an account plan or fields within your CRM system. I like to use a 'Deal Sheet' to obtain relevant information from my research and share and collaborate on it with my colleagues.

The Deal Sheet

You can use your format to do this, but if you want to use The Deal Sheet, you can find a copy in the downloads section of www.meddicc.com.

The Brief - To begin, I find it helps to summarize your engagement so far with the organization and how the opportunity to engage with them came about. For people on your team joining the first call, this will give them a useful context.

Tech Snapshot - If you are selling a technical solution, I find it helpful to capture information about their tech landscape. Not just what technology they use, but if applicable, what kind of metrics can you see? Publicly available information such as how many web hits they get can be useful at this stage.

Participants - List who is attending the call from both sides and what you think each person's role will be.

The Questions - Within your document, you can plan which questions you want to ask. These should be personalized questions rather than generic questions, meaning you start with a blank section for each Deal Sheet.

Anticipated Objections - There are likely some objections that you anticipate going into the call. Highlighting these in the Deal Sheet will help you to effectively handle them if and when they arise.

The Deal Sheet can become a part of the sales process itself; if an SDR has created the opportunity, they can use it as a handover/briefing document for the Seller.

Be Open

At least nine out of every ten of your discovery questions should be open-ended versus closed.

Open-ended questions invite thoughtful answers. They are generally tough to give short answers to. If used correctly, they open up a discussion about a topic. For example, an open-question could be:

"Can you tell me how GDPR impacts your ability to communicate with your customers?"

The likelihood of the customer not giving an insightful answer is unlikely.

Close-ended questions, on the other hand, usually always receive a short response, most frequently "Yes" or "No".

An example of a close-ended question would be:

"Is GDPR impacting your ability to communicate with customers?"

In contrast, close-ended questions should be used sparingly. Not only will they limit the amount of information you get, but being on the other side of them is a pretty miserable experience for your customer. It starts to feel more like an interrogation than a conversation.

A general rule of thumb is to only use a close-ended question if you want an affirmative "Yes" or "No" answer.

An excellent hack to keep your questions open-ended is to use the TED Acronym:

- Could you please **T**ell me about it…
- Can you please **E**xplain to me…
- Would you please **D**escribe how…

Hunt the Negatives

Sellers are often told to stay positive when selling. I think this is awful advice and should be widely ignored. Elite Sellers know that digging into the negative is what turns pain from being indicated to them, to being implicated upon them, thus making them want to solve it immediately.

Discovery is About Them, Not You

Sellers should approach their first call discovery with a consultative mindset. Your job is to discover the lay of the land and if there is a problem here that is worth solving.

A proven method to open up the discussion on the right path in the first call is to ask the customer what it was that made them take the meeting or what they are hoping to get from it. This should give some opening context of what they expect from you and may provide an early clue as to what they hope you could help them solve.

A significant benefit of having done the level of research and planning discussed earlier in this chapter is that you can do discovery in such a relevant manner that the customer is unlikely to feel like they are being taken through a discovery process. When done correctly, it will feel more like a conversation between two people about the organization's goals and challenges. It will instantly elevate you to a position of trust that permits you to do the level of discovery required to uncover the pains that could progress your deal.

Only once you have established that there is a problem painful enough for the customer to want to solve can you then move onto discovering if they will buy from you. This moment represents THE MOST critical point in your discovery process, where you choose to switch from pain discovery mode to deal qualification mode.

Switching from Pain Mode to Qualification Mode

Sellers frequently make the mistake of switching too quickly. They hunt around trying to find the pain and the moment they uncover it, they switch to trying to sell against it. Metaphorically speaking the pain they have discovered is just the smoke rising from a more profound fire. The Seller is so intent on getting the chance to do their pitch that they ignore the potential signs of a more significant fire to uncover and instead, switch into selling their 'smoke removal solution'. If they had stayed in discovery mode, they would have found the fire itself, and the chances are that the fire is burning like an inferno, causing 10x more pain to the organization than that of the smoke.

The customer is much more likely to spend more money to bring in a fire brigade than to solve their relatively minor smoke issue.

The Seller that didn't stop when they found smoke went on to dig deeper once they found the initial pain. When a Seller finds pain and delves deeper into it, the process is called two-sided discovery.

Two-Sided Discovery

Later in this book, within the *Implicate the Pain* chapter, you will learn how important it is to move from identifying pain through to implicating it. Implicating the pain means you make your customer feel the severity of the pain they have, and two-sided discovery plays a big part in this process.

Whereas most Sellers perform one-sided discovery, which is where they ask their customer questions to uncover the pain that their solution can solve, two-sided discovery is where we get our customers to become more conscious of their pain by our process of asking more specific and deeper questions relating to their pain.

An example of a one-sided discovery question versus two-sided is as follows:

One-Sided:

Seller: "Would you say that this issue is making your team less productive?"

Customer: "Yes."

Two-Sided:

Seller: "Are you able to tell me how much less productive you think this issue is making your team?"

Customer: "Hmm, perhaps 20-30%."

At first glance, the main difference between the two questions may seem that one is a closed question, and the other is an open-ended question. This is true, but it is what happens next that defines whether it is one or two-sided. In the example below, we assume both scenarios have come from the two-sided answer to the previous question:

One-Sided:

Seller: "20-30%, that is a lot! If I could help you reduce that, would you be interested in looking more closely at it?"

Customer: "Yes."

Two-Sided:

Seller: "20-30%? That is high, can you explain to me why this is the case?"

Customer: "Well... Not only does it take us longer, but when the process runs, we have to monitor it, so my team can't take on any other tasks."

Seller: "Wow... So, of the 20-30% productivity you are losing, how much of it is because your team is having to keep an eye on the process while it runs?"

Customer: "Maybe over half... 15%?"

Seller: "If you were able to free up 30% of your team's time, what else would they be able to get done?"

Customer: "We looked into this and figured out that we could probably save 3-5 days each month."

Seller: "And how much extra revenue a month would that deliver?"

The more you dig deep into the pain, the causes, and the repercussions, the more your customer will feel implicated by it, and the greater their appetite will be to solve it.

Finish Strong

One of the highest stakes moments in enterprise sales is the conclusion of the first call. The call may represent the amalgamation of hours of work trying to get the customer interested. Depending on how you finish the call will determine whether all those hours of research and preparation was worthwhile. Can you achieve the next steps you want?

The good news is that if you have adequately prepared, you will have readied yourself for this moment and should be prepared to obtain the next step you desire.

However, one thing to be conscious of is that if you ask your customer what they think the next steps should be, they are likely to stop, think, and contemplate the circumstances and then formulate an answer. As you may not have had a chance to build trust with your customer at this point, customers often retreat to the safety of taking the decision offline. They will say:

"We'll debrief internally and get back to you on what we think the next steps should be. Are you able to send us the deck?"

This is not a good outcome as you will have lost the initiative and your deal is now in the hands of your customer.

Instead, try using this hack from former FBI Negotiator Chris Voss, who says that you should simply say:

"It seems like you might have some next steps in mind?"

Voss states that he doesn't know what the science is behind this line, but it seems to remove barriers and tap directly into the customer's thought processes. Voss states that the line "Unlocks the floodgates of truth-telling" and that your customer's thoughts will come streaming out of their mouth. In my experience, this hack works like a Jedi mind trick and circumnavigates any hesitation your customer has to get a solid next step locked in.

If the way of the Jedi is not for you and you want to try a more traditional line, you can simply say something like:

"Thank you for the super insight you have given me today. If it is OK with you, then I think a good next step would be to show you how we can connect our solution to solving some of the goals and challenges you have raised today."

This will have a robust effect on moving your deal towards the next steps you desire.

There is a high likelihood that if you had an opportunity to dig deep with discovery, you will have identified other stakeholders you should be engaging with. In this scenario, be sure to request an introduction by stating that you have heard that other people sound like they may be stakeholders and that you think it is crucial you are introduced to them.

This is Not All Just for the First Call

As I said at the beginning of this chapter, discovery is not something you 'get done'; it is something you continuously do. Therefore, many of the techniques and strategies within this First Call section are critical parts of **all** discovery.

They are included within the First Call section because if they are not deployed correctly within the first call, your chances of progressing to any future stages are severely diminished.

What to do if the Customer isn't Aware of their Problem

If your customer doesn't know they have a problem, they are unaware of how big their problem is, or they know they have one but didn't know it could be solved, then it is your job as the Seller to alert the customer to the problem and the pain it is causing.

The best way to raise the problem's profile is through thorough two-sided discovery focusing on getting the customer to walk you through their operations.

Combine the research you have done with the 7 Big Questions, and you will go on a course to uncover the pain if it is there.

What to do if the Customer is Aware of their Problem

If we are invited by the customer to help them solve a problem they are aware of, it is vital that we run a thorough discovery process as if they aren't aware of the problem.

We have to uncover why the problem is urgent, revealing what is causing it, and what has made the customer want to solve it. If we are following our competition into the deal, then it is likely that they have heavily influenced the Decision Criteria. If they are any good, they will have done so to their strengths and towards our weaknesses. Understanding the lay of the land in these circumstances is crucial.

It may just be the case that the customer has some prior experience at another company with a solution like yours, or they have read online or in an analyst report about solutions like yours. Either way, it is essential that we don't merely settle for the information that is made available to us as, not only could this have been influenced by the competition, but if we simply settle with what we are given, we are missing our chance to change the Decision Criteria towards our strengths and to differentiate ourselves.

Picture your biggest competitor engaging with your ideal customer. In doing so, they have established a Decision Criteria of 10 things that the customer thinks they need from a solution like yours. Upon being brought into the deal, you could take these ten criteria and try to fit your solution against them. However, by doing so, you will be fighting a losing battle as you'll always be second best to your competition's Decision Criteria. Instead, if you engage your customer in a thorough discovery process, you could identify the ten criteria:

- Three of them you can solve for better by doing something only your solution can do.
- Two of them the customer doesn't need.
- Four of them you have a similar ability to do as your competition.
- One of them you are unable to do as well as the competition (Risk identified).
- Four new criteria that only your solution can do, or that you do much better than your competition.

As so often is the case with good discovery, following the above example would increase the trust that your customer has in you. The bonus in this instance is that it is also likely to decrease your customer's trust with your competition – a real win/win situation.

Discovery in the Sales Process

As mentioned at the beginning of this chapter, discovery is not something that you get done. Discovery is something you continuously do; therefore, you can find discovery throughout the stages of your sales process.

Early-Stage:

By using discovery early in your sales process, you will uncover what is essential to your customer. Depending on how the opportunity has arisen with the customer will depend on the mindset of your customer.

If you have approached the customer cold, then your strategy for discovery will likely need to be broad as you scan for pain that they may not be currently aware of (or feel the need to solve).

If the customer has approached you as part of a broader evaluation they are doing, then they are likely to have a better understanding of their pain. However, it will be critical that you dig into their pain via discovery to ascertain the origins of their pain and if any other parties have influenced them.

In the early stages, your customer will be keenly trying to establish their Decision Criteria and determine if your solution can help them solve their problems.

Using the information you have learned, you should be painting a picture back to your customer of how much their current problems are costing them, how you will solve those problems, and what the quantified value your solution will bring. This information should be underpinned with reference points of where you have done this before.

Mid-Stages:

As you move into the mid-stages of your deal, discovery shifts to take a focus on qualifying your position against the MEDDICC of the deal. This entails qualifying your Champion, the Economic Buyer, the Decision Criteria, and the process.

Discovery becomes much more about the lay of the organization's land and finding a consensus that the pain you have found, and the solution you are proposing, is agreed upon with your customer.

Towards the latter part of the mid-stages, you should be using discovery to uncover any unknown parts of the Decision Process and Paper Process.

Late-Stages:

In the late stages, your discovery is likely to be focused on ensuring you are on top of the Decision Process and Paper Process, and that there aren't going to be any surprises such as new stakeholders, new criteria or processes that were unexpected.

In Summary

Discovery is a crucial part of MEDDICC. The strength of how well MEDDICC will work for your deal is almost exclusively related to how good your discovery is.

Good discovery will help you qualify if you should first and foremost be in a deal, and then it'll help you identify value and areas for differentiation.

When deployed correctly, good discovery will build your credibility with your customer as you are focused on their success and winning together.

A word from Jack on Discovery

The key MEDDICC elements to focus on in discovery are Metrics, Implicate the Pain, and Champion.

Learn your Metrics - New Sellers to MEDDICC assume the first element to learn is Implicate the Pain when instead, you should focus on the Metrics as they represent the business outcomes your solution provides. Therefore by knowing your Metrics, you will know what questions to ask in discovery, and be able to offer a viable solution off the bat.

Link the Implicated Pain to an existing initiative - Look for initiatives within the customer's organization to attach your solution.

Talk like a business person - When you talk like a business person trying to solve business problems, a business Champion will emerge. By contrast, if you talk like a technology salesperson, you won't attract a business Champion.

DON'T KNOCK THE COMPETITION

One of the earliest rules I learned in sales was, "Don't knock the competition." The rule states that Sellers shouldn't criticize their competition in front of their customers.

Despite this being one of the oldest rules in sales, I still see and hear stories of Sellers criticizing their competition to their customers.

This chapter is here to impact positive change in our industry and influence 'clean' selling. You will win more by selling clean, and MEDDICC can help.

There are several reasons why it is not a good idea to criticize your competition:

1. It is unprofessional

It can be seen as dishonorable to criticize your competition, which is likely to lower your standing with your customer.

2. You are also criticizing your customer

In a competitive deal where your customer is considering your solution versus your competitor's, by criticizing your competition, you are questioning their judgment. Imagine you were considering buying either a BMW or a Mercedes, and you liked both. If the BMW salesperson started saying how bad the Mercedes was, you could take the criticism personally as it undermines your judgment.

3. It makes you look weak

If you start talking negatively about your competition without being directly invited to do so, you will appear as if you have insecurities about your solution.

4. It focuses on the negative

Your customer isn't going to feel good about having a negative discussion about your competition.

5. Your competition is unlikely to be caught out by your criticism

If you say something negative about your competition, it raises a concern with your customer and they are likely to raise it with your competition, giving them a chance to respond and overcome the issue. If your competition is sharp, they'll rebuff the issue in a manner that shows you up for playing 'dirty'.

I once had a competitor we suspected had paid for some negative PR to be written about our company. The article was about a security flaw that was fixed immediately, but the competition was still using the article over two years later. I genuinely believe that our competitor's use of the article helped us rather than hindered us as it allowed us to do two things:

1. Take the high road - I instated a policy with my sales team that if we ever felt under attack by our competition, we would not respond in kind. Instead, we would say:

> "The issue you have just raised is something we regularly hear our competition saying about us… We are not going to get into a tit for tat debate with our competition. We would rather focus on our suitability for your needs."

This response elevated our position with our customers as being honorable, and as the biblical fable says:

"A lion doesn't concern himself with the opinion of a sheep."

2. Excuse to reference sell - In the above example where our competition was sharing the security flaw article, we would break our response down into three parts:

    i. Explaining what the issue was and how we dealt with it

    ii. Why it was irrelevant now

    iii. Why other brands had chosen us despite having had the same article sent to them. This tactic is particularly effective if you can reference organizations with high-security standards such as banks or government customers.

The last time a customer raised the security flaw article in a meeting, I flipped the conversation to praise our competition. I said:

"I am not going to get into a tit for tat discussion about us and competition name. They have quite a good solution, and sometimes organizations will pick them, and sometimes they will pick us.

One thing we have become very good at is picking the companies that are likely to choose us and specializing in trying to win them as customers.

That is why I am here to support Seller'sname, and you have the full support of my team on this project.

The reason we feel so confident we are the right solution for you is..."

I then listed the unique differentiators that we had identified, quantified, and worked on getting added to the Decision Criteria.

As we left the customer's office, one of the execs from the meeting followed us to the elevators and said:

> *"Hey, I just wanted to say that I really liked what you said when the thing about the competition came up, that was really refreshing."*

We won that deal, and to my best knowledge, my team has never lost a deal to that competitor, where our competition has used the article.

Stay Professional. Use MEDDICC

The intention Sellers have when knocking their competition is to try and highlight weaknesses. Fortunately for those of us that sell with honor, direct criticism doesn't resonate with customers.

However, it doesn't mean that you should skip making your customer aware of the weaknesses of your competition. It just means that you need to take a more professional approach. This is where MEDDICC comes in.

By being thorough in your discovery, you are likely to uncover unique differentiators of your solution. By implicating the pain that your solution solves and attaching the value of solving it to a Metric, you will be in a strong position to have the differentiator added to your customer's Decision Criteria.

What you are doing is turning your differentiators into requirements. The objective is to obtain consensus with your customer that your differentiator is a requirement they need.

In the Qualification Chapter, I described the engagement with the Global Media Company that was looking to buy an enterprise social media platform.

The unique differentiator we identified was the rules engine, which turned out to be the deal's winning factor. The trick was to identify the differentiator, quantify the pain it would solve, and then get it inserted into the Decision Criteria.

In MEDDICC terms, we used discovery to Implicate the Pain, which we then quantified with Metrics and then added to the Decision Criteria by reaching a consensus with the customer that they needed the functionality.

Once you have your differentiator locked into the M, I, and DC of MEDDICC, you can move to put it to work against your competition. The best tactic for doing this comes by way of Trap Setting. You can set your competition up to trap themselves in a shortfall by asking Trap-Setting questions to your customer.

Trap-Setting Questions

Trap-Setting Questions are questions that you ask your customer to uncover or highlight a point of differentiation around your solution that, by proxy, goes on to highlight a shortfall of your competition.

The term was coined by Force Management. The President, John Kaplan, described that the best way to get to a Trap-Setting Question is to focus on a unique differentiator that you have. Once you have this in mind, ask yourself, "So what if the customer doesn't have it?" Once you know the answer to that question, think about what questions you would ask your customer to get them to consider it.

For example: If a sales leader is looking to implement a sales qualification framework and is considering MEDDICC versus BANT, and I want them to buy this book, I would not criticize BANT. Instead, I would ask Trap-Setting Questions aimed at highlighting my strengths and BANT's weaknesses. The questions may sound like:

Me: "What are you doing to ensure you are qualifying your deals throughout their lifecycle?"

Sales Leader: "We are not qualifying our deals very well at the moment, least of all throughout the lifecycle."

Me: "Ok, but if you do invest in implementing a qualification framework, will you want it to help you qualify throughout the entirety of your deal lifecycle?"

Sales Leader: "Yes, definitely!"

Me: "Do you mind if I add this as part of your Decision Criteria?"

Sales Leader: "Please do."

In this three-question exchange, I have not only uncovered a Pain, but I have also turned the Pain into a requirement that sits within the Decision Criteria. Of course, the work here isn't complete. As detailed in the Decision Criteria chapter, there is a skill in adding your own requirements to the Decision Criteria, but this is a solid way to start.

It is important to remember that Trap-Setting Questions are not intended to trap your customer; they are intended to trap your competition. They are called Traps because, like a trap, you set them up for your competition to fall into.

Continuing on the above example of where a Sales Leader is looking for a sales qualification framework, let's imagine a likely conversation that the BANT Seller is now going to have:

Sales Leader: "How does BANT help me to qualify throughout the sales process?"

BANT Seller: "BANT helps you to qualify at the earliest opportunity. Once you know the customer has a Budget, Authority, a Need, and their Timing, you are qualified!"

Sales Leader: "Hmm, ok."

If you are a Seller representing MEDDICC in the above example, you have laid the foundations perfectly for yourself to double down on the differentiator you have identified for yourself. Even if BANT is a superior qualification framework for early qualification, it is unlikely it would prevail over MEDDICC; such is the power of the trap we have set.

(BANT isn't a superior early qualification framework, just sayin'.)

Trap-Setting Guidelines

As a Seller, I initially found it tricky to get my head around Trap-Setting. I felt a little like I was acting a play for which my fellow actor didn't have the same script as me. I'd ask questions and not get the answers I needed.

Trap-Setting is an elite-level strategy. Just like any skill level-related pursuit, it takes practice and perseverance. Thinking you'll come out of the blocks setting Trap-Setting questions perfectly would be the same as a person expecting to apply topspin on their backhand perfectly on their first try in a game of tennis.

This section looks at some guidelines to improve your Trap-Setting:

Persevere and Practice

Trap-Setting may not click at first, but keep at it. Practice will make perfect.

Don't (only) practice on your customers.

This is where we can break the rule of 'do not practice on your customers' a bit because you need real-world experience with Trap-Setting, and there is not too much that can go wrong if you are not very good at it. So, get out there and try it out.

However, you should also practice with your peers. It is likely that as a sales team, you will be able to construct some themes for your Trap-Setting questions for each competitor. So, I'd advise getting together to brainstorm some likely traps you can lay for your most commonly found Competitors.

Keep it Open

Like any good discovery question, you need to keep the questions open-ended. Consider the above example with the Sales Leader considering MEDDICC and BANT if the opening question was:

> *"Are you qualifying your deals throughout their lifecycle?"*

The answer would have been "No" and it would have been much harder to get where I wanted to go from there, not to mention it would have felt more like an interrogation than a conversation for the customer.

Keep it Two-Sided

We want to use Trap-Setting to set up our competition to fall into our traps and make our customers consider the repercussions of the shortfall we are highlighting.

Again, using the MEDDICC vs. BANT example, not only will the Seller benefit from finding out about the lack of deal qualification within their deal cycles, but the customer will also be forced to consider the issue; and at that moment, will feel the pain implicated upon them.

Take Action

If you have asked a good Trap-Setting question that has hit the mark but not followed through with your customer by asking them to add it to their Decision Criteria, then proverbially speaking, you will have pulled back the springs of your trap but have left it in a safe place far away from any likelihood of your competition falling into it.

Summary of Trap-Setting

When done effectively, Trap-Setting Questions should open your customer's mind to the possibilities with your solution for aspects of value that they hadn't perhaps considered yet.

Trap-Setting Questions also have the by-product similar to two-sided discovery, where they make your customer feel Implicated by the intensity of the pain and, therefore, may have the effect of increasing the urgency surrounding your deal. Best of all, they do this while simultaneously highlighting a shortfall of your competition's solution without you needing to lower your integrity to criticize your competitor directly.

Win/Win/Win.

PRICE CONDITIONING

In enterprise sales, it is rare for an organization to know with any accuracy what a solution like yours will cost them.

Unless they have received guidance from a competitor or someone within their organization who has purchased a solution like yours, often they will not know what the likely cost will be.

If you don't believe me, then consider the situation for yourself. The chances are your current role isn't the first you have had in your industry, but did you know the cost of your technology at any time before you saw the price list? Chances are you didn't, and you will have known far more than a customer does.

This means that you, as the Seller, are most likely going to be the person to set the expectation of the cost, and wherever you set that expectation, the customer will anchor themselves.

Therefore, it is important that you work to set an expectation of price with your customer. If you don't, then someone else will, and you will not only have missed an opportunity to own the cost expectation, but the expectation could be set lower than where your price is likely to be, which instantly makes your solution expensive.

As crazy as it may sound, it is often that simple. Your customer's perception of cost is often left wide open, just waiting for someone to set expectations.

For this reason, a highly effective strategy is to deploy what is called 'Price Conditioning'. This is a process where you give your customer information leading towards setting an expectation whereby the price is likely to be higher than it will be.

You most certainly will have experienced the psychology behind this yourself as a consumer where you anticipated something would cost more than it turned out to cost. You will recall the positive feeling that you felt; you will have felt delighted by what seemed to be a low cost. The reality is, it may well be a very average, or even a high price, but you had been price conditioned to expect it to be higher, and voila! It seems low and, therefore, 'cheap' to you.

In the connected world we live in today where information is just a couple of taps away, price conditioning is much less effective than it once was. However, in enterprise sales, it still holds its own. It is so challenging for customers to assume the cost of something due to the complexity and variation of one solution to another.

Elite Sellers use this to their advantage by ensuring they set the expectation of cost as being high with their customers by price conditioning. There are many methods in which you can deploy price conditioning. I have listed a few of my favorites below:

The Reference-Based Price Condition

When you refer to a customer and the successful results they have had from your solution, then use this to price condition by saying something along the lines of:

"When ACME INC implemented our solution, they saw the lifetime value of their customers rise by 25%, which meant an additional $20m of annual revenue. The size of their deployment of our solution is similar to yours, and I am sure you wouldn't mind paying us $500,000 a year if it meant you, too, could get an additional $20m of revenue, right?"

The Casual Drop Price Condition

When you have the opportunity to drop a number into the conversation subtly, you do so; only the number is a price set to raise their expectation of the cost. You could do this with a question, for example, you could be asking about the Decision Process and say something like:

> *"Do you have any varying authorization levels based on different cost amounts? For example, if our solution was to cost over $500,000, does it need to go through any additional decision-makers first?"*

The Pricing Model Price Condition

When you are starting to work on the scope of the deal with your customer, you can use the process of explaining your pricing model as a price conditioning exercise. For example:

> *"Our pricing model works via the number of calls you make on our servers. Based on your numbers, if you continue to grow as you have over the last 12 months, the price could be as much as $500,000 more than it would be on last year's volumes."*

The Pricing Model Price Condition can also be used when talking about deployment size or different modules too.

Other methods of price conditioning can be as subtle as filling out the 'cost' section within the Go-Live Plan.

When done consistently and thoroughly, by the time your customer gets your proposal, they will be expecting a higher cost. Therefore, your price will seem low, and this is all before they've even started to negotiate.

I am often asked what happens if the customer reacts negatively to the price conditioning exercise. Usually, people will ask something like:

"What if the customer says 'forget it as we cannot afford that amount'?"

Believe it or not, this is a wonderful thing to happen. It means your price condition has landed and taken effect. In an instance like this, I would advise the Seller to simply say something like:

"Oh no, I don't know how much this will cost for you. We are yet to crunch the numbers. I was only giving that number as an example."

I have heard some people refer to this process as anchoring. I prefer the term price conditioning as anchoring tends to be about negotiating and setting out your starting point.

Price conditioning is more around the psychology of the buyer's journey.

Good news though, reader, is our solution is only going to cost $300,000, which is $200,000 less than what this chapter had price conditioned you to believe. Why? Because we have consistently been mentioning the amount of $500,000.

THE GO-LIVE PLAN

The Go-Live Plan is a tool Elite Sellers use to plan through the Decision and Paper Processes with their customer. The origins of the Go-Live Plan come from the 'Close Plan', which is a document that enterprise Sellers have been using for decades to present their interpretation of the steps ahead of themselves to get their deal closed.

I most frequently see Close Plans used internally to sales organizations because the language is focused on the Seller's goals and not the buyer's. After all, who likes to be 'closed'?

Using a Close Plan internally misses two huge opportunities for the Seller. The first is the chance for the Seller to obtain consensus from the customer about the stage they are at and the stages ahead of them. The second is by making it a one-sided document that the buyer has very little input into its direction.

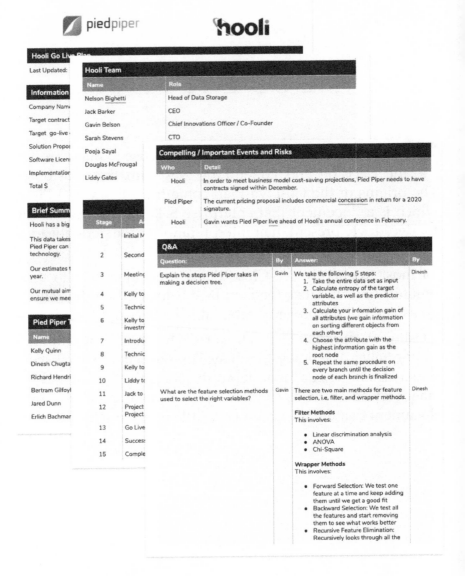

Introducing the Go Live Plan

The Go-Live Plan is different. It's a collaborative, live document of which these are the main differences and benefits of it:

1. It is customer-focused: It is written in the language of the customer, not the Seller. The Seller cares about the contract date, the customer cares about the go live date.

As the document is called a 'Go-Live Plan', its goal is to get the customer to go live with your solution. The final stage is the 'go live' stage, not the 'close'.

That said, whilst you may use the Go-Live Plan after your deal is signed, it is likely that your organization has an entirely different (and more proficient) process in place to progress the customer from going through the implementation stages towards their go live, however, the rationale for looking further ahead has two benefits:

1. It eradicates the feeling the customer is likely to get with a 'Close Plan' where it seems the Seller is only interested in getting their deal 'closed'. The focus of a Go-Live Plan is getting the solution live!

2. The Go-Live Plan is most effectively used when planning backwards from a targeted Go Live date. Working backward from a deadline takes us to our second major benefit of using a Go-Live Plan:

2. Go-Live Plan Inspires Urgency: Working backwards from a Go Live date inspires urgency and as you map out all of the stages with your Champion, you will identify together when the deal is likely to hit important milestones such as engagement with the legal, security, and procurement teams. Identifying these steps earlier in the process and uncovering from your Champion how long each engagement will take can radically enhance your ability as a Seller to accurately forecast your deal as well as inspiring your Champion to accelerate engagement with those teams once they see how much their processes will impact the timeline towards going live.

9	Kelly to send MSA	Kelly	12/06/20	No
10	Liddy to review/respond to MSA	Liddy	12/11/20	No
11	Jack to sign Pied Piper Contracts	Jack	12/20/20	No
12	Project Kick-Off with Project Manager & Project Team	Nelson & Jared	3/1/21	No
13	Go Live	Nelson	1/18/21	No
14	Success Team Kick-Off	Jared	1/18/21	No
15	Completion of Case Study	Jared	3/24/21	No

3. Go Live is the best place for *stuff*: Throughout the course of a deal, Sellers and buyers share a huge amount of information with each other. Much of this information is shared in document format and gets passed via email where it stays for reference. Elite Sellers surface the information into the Go-Live Plan by adding relevant information to the fields of the document, as well as adding links to any useful documents such as the proposal or business case within the Go-Live Plan.

This improves the selling experience for the customer who now has just one place to go to find all important information and documentation, but it also has one major added bonus which is that it means the Go-Live Plan is more likely to be visited by the customer to obtain the information and links it contains, subsequently bringing them to the Go-Live Plan where they are likely to digest any updates and potentially even make their own updates.

Many Elite Sellers will use the top information section of their Go-Live Plan to display information to the customer. This is a great place to Price Condition your customer with your estimated cost earlier in the deal cycle.

4. Go-Live Plan is Collaborative: The Go-Live Plan is most effectively deployed in a live state. This means that only one version exists that can be updated in real-time by all people with access to it.

At the time of printing, Google Documents is the best solution for this purpose as it is not only easy to use and share, but it is also widely adopted enough that there is rarely a barrier to entry for the customer to use it.

Google Documents is also useful as you can tag other users with comments and questions on parts of the Go-Live Plan.

Kelly	11/26/20	YES
Sarah	12/05/20	In Progress
Kelly	12/06/20	No
Liddy	12/11/20	No
Jack	12/20/20	No
Nelson & Jared	3/1/21	No

Kelly Quinn
09:59 Today ✓

sarah@hooli.com - Are you please able to confirm the technical validation as per our discussion earlier today?

In the most successful instances, your customer will collaborate on the Go-Live Plan with you. They will update the stages and timeframes themselves and take ownership of tasks and milestones.

Your Champion will help you ensure the plan is accurate and shared internally with all stakeholders.

5. Make it the Home for Questions: Whilst this benefit could easily fall under the former two benefits, it is such a strong benefit when used correctly that it deserves its own section:

Throughout the course of your deal, the customer will ask a number of questions through a number of channels—from in-person to calls and email. Capturing all of these questions and adding them to a 'Q&A' part of your Go-Live Plan has three distinct benefits:

1. It is convenient for your customer - they know they can go to the Go-Live Plan to find the Q&A

2. Answering questions in a document allows you to link to supporting documentation, or to include graphics within your answer

3. It builds trust as there is an easy to find and auditable list of questions that have been asked and their answers

4. It allows Sellers to follow up on important questions that were asked and engage other stakeholders from both sides to weigh in on the response

The benefits of The Go-Live Plan, in summary, are centered towards increasing visibility of the current status and future stages of your deal whilst also increasing communication and collaboration around it.

Buyers working with Sellers using a Go-Live Plan benefit from a streamlined and convenient method to exchange information whilst also being exposed to the time-related urgency that having dates, milestones, and deadlines against stages.

When Should You Share Your Go-Live Plan With Your Customer?

The short answer to this question is: At the earliest possible opportunity.

The more detailed answer is that you want to look for buying signals before introducing the Go-Live Plan. If you introduce it before the customer has shifted their mind to the possibility of buying from you, then it is likely to have an adverse effect and backfire.

I have seen Go-Live Plans presented at the end of a good first meeting. The Seller used it to illustrate what an engagement looks like with them, what the customer can expect from them; a consultative approach, efficient responses to requests, a business case, etc. They also use it as an opportunity to qualify the stakeholders on what role they will play (Champion, Economic Buyer, Coach, etc.) as well as setting out some expectations from the Seller's side around reasonable response times and which channels are preferred for communication.

How to Build Your Go-Live Plan

Personalization Goes Far

The less this looks like the selling organization's document, the better. My advice is at the least to make the colors neutral. Elite Sellers may alter the styling to make it fall in line with the branding of the customer. This will help them see it as their document and not yours and could increase their likelihood to participate in collaborating within it.

Hooli Go Live Plan		
Last Updated:	Thursday 26th November 2020	By: Kelly Quinn

Adding the customer's logo next to yours at the top and personalizing the header to say the customer's name are just a couple of small tweaks that go a long way.

The Information Header

Within the top bank of information, this is your chance to set out information as you see it and request confirmation from your customer. Again, make sure you personalize these sections to not just your own terminologies, but your customer's too.

Information	
Company Name	Hooli
Target contractual signing date	Tuesday 22nd December 2020
Target go-live date	Monday 18th January 2021
Solution Proposed	Pied Piper Compression Cloud
Software Licenses	$545,000
Implementation Services	$128,000
Total $	$673,000

This is the section you can set your stool out for a *Targeted Close Date* as well as the cost of your solution, giving you an early chance to set expectations and Price Conditions.

The Brief Summary

This is a chance for you to briefly articulate your understanding of the engagement. Brief being the key term, your job here is to construct a summary that captures 'the why' of your engagement, as well as any information that is relevant to both the most engaged stakeholder and the stakeholder who arrives in the final stages.

> **Brief Summary**
>
> Hooli has a big amount of data, not just big data, but big little data. A lot of data.
>
> This data takes up a big amount of storage space costing Hooli in excess of $22,000,000 a month, Pied Piper can significantly reduce the amount of data Hooli stores via our Compression Cloud technology.
>
> Our estimates the monthly cost of $22,000,000 will be reduced by 69% saving Hooli $15,000,000 a year.
>
> Our mutual aim is to have Pied Piper live by mid-January. This document serves as a mutual plan to ensure we meet that goal.

The Teams

This is the section where you can identify who the stakeholders are on both sides.

Within your team section, it is a great opportunity for you to highlight the resources you will be aligning to the engagement, both pre and post-sales. I advise highlighting as early as you can who the post-sales team will be that will be supporting the customer towards going live, as well as any more senior executives that could act as a sponsor for the project.

Pied Piper Team		
Name	Email	Role
Kelly Quinn	kelly@piedpiper.com	Account Executive
Dinesh Chugtai	dinesh@piedpiper.com	Co-CTO / Sales Engineer
Richard Hendricks	richard@piedpiper.com	CEO / Executive Sponsor
Bertram Gilfoyle	gilfoyle@piedpiper.com	Co-CTO / Systems Architect
Jared Dunn	jared@piedpiper.com	Customer Success Manager
Erlich Bachman	erlich@piedpiper.com	Chief Evangelist Officer

An Elite move is to invite all of your team to open the document when you share it with your customer so that they can see your full team active within it.

For the customer's Section, this is a great chance for the Seller to qualify who the stakeholders within the project will be and what their roles will be.

Hooli Team	
Name	**Role**
Nelson Bighetti	Head of Data Storage
Jack Barker	CEO
Gavin Belson	Chief Innovations Officer / Co-Founder
Sarah Stevens	CTO
Pooja Sayal	Chief Data Officer
Douglas McFrougal	Procurement Manager
Liddy Gates	Senior Legal Counsel

Remember, this is a customer-facing document, and as tempting as it will be to highlight your Champion's role as 'Champion' within this document, it is actually likely to have a negative effect as the Champion may be seen as biased.

Planned Steps and Key Events

As they say, "This is where the magic happens". It is within this section that you can detail out your understanding of every step, stage, and key event that is ahead of you and your customer in your journey towards going live.

	Planned Steps and key events in Go Live			
Stage	**Action (*Denotes Important Steps)**	**Owner**	**By When**	**Complete?**
1	Initial Meeting	Kelly	10/15/20	YES
2	Second Meeting	Kelly	11/05/20	YES
3	Meeting with Technical Team	Dinesh	11/10/20	YES
4	Kelly to present the proposed solution	Kelly	11/20/20	YES
5	Technical Deep Dive	Nelson	11/24/20	YES
6	Kelly to present projected return on investment/business case	Kelly	11/25/20	YES
7	Introduction to Procurement	Kelly	11/26/20	YES
8	Technical Sign off	Sarah	12/05/20	In Progress
9	Kelly to send MSA	Kelly	12/06/20	No
10	Liddy to review/respond to MSA	Liddy	12/11/20	No
11	Jack to sign Pied Piper Contracts	Jack	12/20/20	No
12	Project Kick-Off with Project Manager & Project Team	Nelson & Jared	3/1/21	No
13	Go Live	Nelson	1/18/21	No
14	Success Team Kick-Off	Jared	1/18/21	No
15	Completion of Case Study	Jared	3/24/21	No

Kelly Quinn
09:59 Today

sarah@hooli.com - Are you please able to confirm the technical validation as per our discussion earlier today?

There are five fields to this section:

1. The Stage

As simple as this column may seem, it is also important as it calls out the order of events. Keeping the plan in order helps to maintain its accuracy. It will also help you reference certain points, for instance, you could ask your customer:

"I have the introduction to Procurement down as stage 7, is that correct? Are there any other stages that have to come before it? And are the stages afterwards correct?"

2. The Action

This column is self-explanatory as should be the contents within it. You will want anyone reading this to have a clear understanding of what each action is. Steer clear from any terms that may cause anyone confusion such as internal language that either side uses, especially three-letter acronyms. Keeping the document open and easy to read will encourage collaboration and input from other stakeholders.

Pro Tip: Backdate activity in the Go-Live Plan to your first engagement. It will remind the customer of all of the work you have both invested to that point and will give the impression of a document that is alive. It will instantly be easier for your customer to understand if they see how it has been completed to that point.

3. The Owner

Delegating responsibility of an action to an owner helps maintain accountability and collaboration throughout the Go-Live Plan.

Pro Tip: Tag the individual using Google Documents' comment functionality to alert them to the delegation of an action. Good practice would be to add a polite message with some context.

It is also useful to tag stakeholders against actions for updates or input on a particular part of the Go-Live Plan.

4. By When

The 'By When' column is for setting a deadline of when the action needs to be completed by.

Ideally, you will work with your Champion backwards from a targeted Go-Live date, or an alternative future goal date and your Champion should help you estimate the amount of time needed for each action.

This column is a powerful tool for helping you to drive urgency and time accountability to stakeholders.

5. The Status

This section helps you to keep track of progress against each action. Similar to the deadline, it will help drive progress and accountability as nobody likes having a red 'No' against their actions.

The Compelling/Important Events and Risks Section

Use this section to call out any major factors such as Compelling or Important Events as well as any Risks that you have identified.

Compelling / Important Events and Risks	
Who	Detail
Hooli	In order to meet business model cost-saving projections, Pied Piper needs to have contracts signed within December.
Pied Piper	The current pricing proposal includes commercial concession in return for a 2020 signature.
Hooli	Gavin wants Pied Piper live ahead of Hooli's annual conference in February.

The Q&A Section

Use this section to capture questions that your customer has and their answers. This serves two purposes: the first is that, over the course of a sales cycle, there are likely to be hundreds of questions asked, many of which the customer will want to refer back to for answers. By keeping the questions and answers in one place, it is convenient for your customer and serves the second purpose which is that it helps make the Go-Live Plan a more useful and 'sticky' document which will go on to increase the likelihood that your customer will visit and contribute to the document.

Q&A			
Question:	By	Answer:	By
What are the feature selection methods used to select the right variables?	Gavin	There are two main methods for feature selection, i.e, filter, and wrapper methods.	Dinesh
		Filter Methods This involves: • Linear discrimination analysis • ANOVA • Chi-Square	
		Wrapper Methods This involves: • Forward Selection: We test one feature at a time and keep adding	

The Levels of Participation

You are likely to find that different customers and individuals will participate differently within the Go-Live Plan. From my experience, they tend to fall into three categories:

The Ideal User

The Ideal User is the customer who uses the document as it is intended to be used—as a tool to keep track of progress towards a Go-Live date and to communicate and collaborate towards that goal within. This type of user keeps their actions up to date and updates other sections as relevant. When they have a question, they add it to the Q&A section and tag you to answer it.

The View User

The View User reads and checks in on the Go-Live Plan regularly but rarely updates it. They leave the updates for you to make.

The Absent User

The Absent User rarely looks at the Go-Live Plan, if at all. This may be for a number of reasons and it is important that you get to the bottom of what the rationale for their lack of cooperation is. The common reasons are:

- **Personality type** - They aren't very organized or they are not fond of these types of approaches. This is OK, but it is important that you find an alternative manner of keeping on top of the Decision and Paper Processes with this type of person.

- **Technical type** - This user can't use Google Documents either from their own technical proficiency or due to guidelines from the organization they work for. As with the Personality type, it is important that you find an alternative method to keep on top of the Decision and Paper Processes.

- **The Unqualified type** - This has little to do with the Go-Live Plan itself and more to do with the customer not being qualified to be at this stage of the deal with you. It could be that you need to work on building a Champion or it could be a red flag that you should be qualifying out as there isn't a real opportunity here. Either way, you have more work to do!

Summary

In an enterprise sales process, there is very little downside in using a Go-Live Plan. A worst-case scenario is that the customer refuses to use it and you identify that they are unqualified or you re-qualify them and realize that they have a technical issue of adversity to the document itself. In this instance, what you have to fall back on is a Close Plan which is what most Sellers should be using to manage the close anyway.

The upside to a Go-Live Plan is that it can keep your deal on track. If executed well, it can be like applying lubrication to those rails to make your deal fly through the stages with no surprises and subsequent time slips.

Finally, if your deal is well qualified, then your customer will benefit from the Go-Live Plan just as much as you do and they will appreciate the professionalism in which you manage the process.

A true win/win situation.

METRICS

Metrics are the quantifiable measures of value that your solution can provide.

The best way I have seen Metrics broken down is how the folks at Sales MEDDIC Group articulate them, which is to split Metrics into two kinds:

Metrics 1 (M1's) - Metrics Proof Points

These are the business outcomes you have delivered for your existing customers.

A quick hack to uncover what the M1's could be is to consider yourself with your customer six months from now in a Quarterly Business Review (QBR). What positive business outcomes would you expect to see from your solution?

For example, if you are selling Sales Analytics Software to sales leaders, in the QBR, they are likely to look at a Metric like forecast accuracy. This, therefore, could become an M1 in your deal.

The best way to introduce M1's is to reference existing customers who benefit from them. This is effective for two reasons:

The first is that it allows you to introduce a customer reference at the earliest opportunity. Demonstrating via social proofing how you have a customer enjoying success with your solution.

The second is that it allows you to talk about how you took an existing customer from a negative status to a positive one, which saves you from criticizing the customer you are selling to. As Jack Napoli would say, "Call someone else's baby ugly before you tell them their baby is ugly."

Metrics 2 (M2's) - Return on Investment

Through effective research, discovery, and by building a consensus with your Champion, you can shift from M1's, which are hypothetical, into M2's, which are specifically curated in collaboration with your customer based upon quantifying the value your solution will provide, AKA the Return on Investment (ROI).

As technology solutions have evolved in recent decades, so has the manner in which you compile Metrics. For instance, the invention of SaaS flipped the business models of technology vendors on their heads, making it become imperative that vendors focus on the success of their customers with their solutions as, without this success, the customer will not renew their license subscriptions.

However, Metrics aren't simply KPIs of your solution's success; they exist to help the Seller and customer build the business case for investment into the solution.

Another way to work out the Metrics is to work backwards from the customer's goals, establishing what it is they are focused on improving. How your solution contributes towards this goal should be something you are able to quantify and, therefore, can become a Metric.

An example of this could be if you are representing a solution that analyzes the performance of websites. If the customer has a goal to increase revenue and you discover an opportunity to improve their page load times, which will subsequently improve their conversion rate, you could surface this as a Metric. This Metric could then be quantified in a business case, i.e. Our Metric of improving load times will increase the conversion rate by 4% which will result in $30m of incremental revenue.

Metrics and Discovery

A mistake that is frequently made is that salespeople align the Metrics to their value proposition. You should take caution with this approach as you will be aligning with your strengths and not your customer's needs.

This is why discovery is critical. Without discovery, you will be in the dark when it comes to uncovering your customer's Metrics.

Within the discovery Process, I recommend trying to uncover your customer's key initiatives. However, be patient, take your time, and go deep to reveal as much information as you can. Do not switch to sales mode; there will be plenty of time for that later.

Salespeople often raise the concern that if they don't start selling soon enough, the opportunity may not progress. My response to this is straightforward—don't engage in opportunities where you feel as though you are walking a tight rope of engagement from the customer. It is always hard for salespeople to qualify out, especially when they think they have genuine value to offer. Still, if you are being forced to sell before uncovering real pains, goals, or challenges, then you are wasting your time. The only way to solve this situation is to find Pain, and if you aren't being given a chance to do that, go and work with a customer who deserves your expertise.

Metrics and Clarity

Having clarity around the Metrics is crucial; they need to be easily understandable to every stakeholder, not just your Champion. One of the most important is the Economic Buyer, meaning the Metrics will have to be in a language that relates to their key initiatives while also satisfying other stakeholders such as the Technical Buyer who is more focused on the how over the why.

Be sure to check the language of your Metrics to ensure they are applicable and understandable to the relevant stakeholders.

Metrics and Urgency

Metrics should be used to drive urgency with your customers.

Elite enterprise sales organization, App Dynamics, tackled this brilliantly by ensuring their Sellers leave every meeting with three questions answered:

The Three Whys:

1. Why should you buy Application Management?

2. Why should you buy from App Dynamics?

3. Why should you buy now?

In the above three questions, Metrics are essential to under-pinning positive intent in questions 1 & 3; they help to quanti-fy the solution's value. They can support the business case that states why the customer should invest now.

However, question number two is where you need to dig deep to uncover Metrics. These will be what differentiates a decision to buy your solution, a competitor's, or if the answers to question number two and three combined aren't strong enough, the customer will do nothing.

My favorite way to uncover Metrics that differentiate is to think about how your solution is uniquely helping your exist-ing customers.

- What does your solution do that is unique, and subse-quently, so is the value?

- What is the Metric that quantifies that value?

This is genuinely a Win/Win situation; you not only under-pin your solution with more value, but by doing so, you set yourself apart from your competitor's solutions.

Metrics and Storytelling

A good story can transfix anyone, and while facts are hard to remember, psychologist Jerome Bruner's research suggests that facts are 20 times more likely to be remembered if they're part of a story.

Using storytelling in your selling to illustrate Metrics is a perfect way of explaining how your solution provides measur-able value. Still, it also allows you to describe how a customer is obtaining the same value. This creates credibility via social proofing and paints a picture in the head of your buyer of a real-life scenario.

Combining great discovery to uncover Metrics that represent the value you can provide, underpinned by customer references detailing how you have delivered the same Metrics to other customers is an elite way of making your customer envisage their future with your solution.

Metrics and Success Criteria

Metrics can often capture the criteria that define your solution as a success; therefore, they can be seen as similar. However, Success Criteria is a term used more broadly and should always be defined. For example, occasionally, deals will require a test of some kind within the sales process. This is often called a Proof of Concept (POC), trial, pilot, or test. It is imperative for the success of your deal that you underpin this test with a 'Success Criteria,' meaning you set out with a goal in mind and some data points you are trying to achieve.

The Success Criteria and Metrics on your deal **aren't** intrinsically linked. They could be related, but often the test serves a different purpose to the main objective of buying your solution. With this in mind, you must establish early on the specifics of any kind of test, and what exactly it is that you are trying to test, and what a successful test would look like.

Once you have this information, you can build the vision of success into a Success Criteria, which should be measurable as the outcome of tests isn't often binary, and you need to remove any uncertainty that opens the results up to interpretation.

Metrics and Go-Live Plan

Metrics should occupy their section of your Go-Live Plan featuring prominently so stakeholders see them. In addition to this, you should structure events expressly to agree upon a consensus of the Metrics.

Metrics and Procurement

By the time you engage with Procurement, you should have your Metrics wholly locked down and validated by your customer. If you are engaging with Procurement before having the universal buy-in of your value, you need to **STOP** and work on getting it. Otherwise, Procurement is likely to knock chunks out of your proposal, and you won't have any reasonable defense at your disposal.

As the legendary FBI Negotiator, Chris Voss, would say:

"We've got to slow things down to speed them up".

Do not overlook Metrics with Procurement

If you have your Metrics locked down, then be sure to make them a prominent part of your conversations with Procurement. I regularly see that, despite a great deal of effort, having been required to get a deal to a point of where Procurement is engaged, Sellers often tend to switch their focus away from the Metrics, Decision Criteria, and Pain and instead zoom in on the Decision and Paper Processes. This is a mistake that will cost your deal size and time to close.

Be on the front foot with Procurement

In your first engagement with Procurement, you should ensure that an agenda item focuses on briefing them on your engagement so far. The Metrics should underpin this part of the agenda, and you should share any supporting documentation ahead of the call to support your Metrics-based conversation.

An example of what happens if you are on your back foot

If you haven't convinced Procurement of your value and they stall the deal, I regularly see Sellers deploy a tactic where they will relate time lost to value lost. For example, they'll say:

"Our Metrics predict that for each week you don't implement our solution, you are losing $100,000 revenue which exceeds the amount you are trying to negotiate!"

A strong point, but don't expect to be the first person to play this angle, and it's likely to be met with a negative response, perhaps something like:

"If I skip running a thorough Procurement process with every bit of technology put in front of me just because it has a positive ROI, we'd get ourselves into a real mess."

Avoid the likelihood of this issue occurring by leading all conversations with Metrics; Procurement wants to get deals done. If you give them compelling information, my experience is that they are much more amicable to work with.

Metrics and Your Sales Process

Metrics play a crucial role throughout your sales process. They are utilized differently at each stage and should evolve as you uncover more information from discovery with new stakeholders.

Early-Stages:

Early in your sales process, Metrics can help you build credibility with your customers. You can combine storytelling and the results you've had with other customers to make a positive picture of your value. To do this, you need to uncover your customer's pains and relate them to where you have solved the same problems before for other customers.

If you can, it is most useful to use comparative Metrics from customers who are ideally similar in their business model and industry.

It can be helpful to refer to Metrics you build from proof-points with other customers as Metrics 1's (M1's).

When used well early in the sales cycle, Metrics do three things:

1) Gives you credibility from the references you've made to other customers and their Metrics.

2) Helps you quantify the Pain that you are trying to solve, helping to Implicate the Pain upon your customer.

3) Broadens your value if you can uncover a Pain that wasn't previously considered and align it to a Metric.

Early Consensus:

At the earliest opportunity, you want to get a consensus on the Metrics with your Champion. The sooner you do this, the sooner you will set the standard that you are selling based on Measurable success and, therefore, appear more credible. You'll also confirm whether your early assumptions are accurate.

Mid-Stages:

Metrics at the mid-stage of your sales cycle is the moment your Metrics come into their own, despite most Sellers never realizing it. At the mid-stage, your customers will be carefully evaluating your solution, potentially against your Competitors, and always against other priorities and projects. This is the time where your Metrics need to be bulletproof.

Mid Consensus:

At the mid-stage, there is a good chance that your customer is evaluating Metrics from other providers, so consensus becomes more important than ever. By this stage, you and your Champion should aim to have a full agreement on how you will measure your solution's success.

Late-Stages:

In the later stages of the sales cycle, the Metrics you have aligned with the project are likely to be evaluated by new stakeholders that have been brought into the Decision Process. Expect your Metrics to come under fresh scrutiny directed at uncovering their accuracy.

You may see new executives brought in to evaluate your business case as well as requests from your customer to have reference calls with other customers, in which the Metrics are likely to be a reference point. How you prepare for this eventuality is essential. Is your Champion briefed and ready to explain the value of your solution? Have you armed them with Metrics to back it up? Generally, by this point, good Sellers have built a proposal to support their deal, but the proposal often becomes outdated as the scope shifts or the commercials alter. For this reason, Elite Sellers keep the proposal up to date and go to the effort to create a summary proposal for more senior executives that covers the main selling points in a clear, easy-to-digest format regardless of who the stakeholder is.

Late Consensus:

At the late stages of your deal, the Metrics act to reinforce and underpin your value, reducing any perception of Risk that may be outstanding.

By this stage, it is imperative that not just your Champion, but also the Economic Buyer and any other significant stakeholders have consensus on the Metrics.

Summary Snapshot of Metrics in the Sales Process:

- Early: How much will this help me? Do I believe you?
- Mid: How much does this value compare to others?
- Late: Have they proven that this value is available?

Metrics After You've Won the Deal

Once the deal is won, Elite Sellers stay engaged on the project, ensuring success because they know that the more credible your Metrics are, the more likely you are to win. There is no better way of building credibility into your Metrics than by references from other customers.

I know of one Elite Seller who, from staying engaged with his deal post-signature, was able to identify that within the customer's first full month of using his solution, he generated enough additional profit to pay for his solution's entire annual cost. Imagine how compelling that anecdote has been for him!

Metrics and Post-Sales

It is common that once you have closed a deal that you pass the ownership of the relationship with your customer to your post-sales team, often a Customer Success Manager, Support team, or an Account Manager.

This passing of the baton often plays a critical part in dictating how successful the customer will go on to be with your solution.

If the pre and post-sales organizations are aligned, passing over a customer who has clearly defined Metrics will be incredibly beneficial to the post-sales team.

We know how important it is for a Seller's success to have successful customers as references; therefore, Elite Sellers always ensure that the handover process to Post-Sales is as thorough as possible.

Capture the Success

The most elite sales organizations focus on capturing success from their clients. Elite Sellers will be tuned into these initiatives to ensure that their customers' success is captured into proof points that are available to be used as references, case studies, quotes, or in any relevant collateral marketing support.

Summary of Metrics

There are many parts of a Seller's job that can be perceived by the buyer as self-serving. However, Metrics is one selling element that the buyer can never feel aggrieved at the Seller for being enthusiastic about. The purpose of Metrics orientates around measuring the success your solution will provide. With this in mind, Sellers should be ruthless in their pursuit of obtaining and agreeing on Metrics into their deals.

As legendary Sales trainer and President of Force Management, John Kaplan, would say:

> *"Small problems receive big discounts, and big problems receive small discounts."*

Metrics are what will help you quantify how big the problem is that you are solving.

A word from Jack on Metrics

Sellers need to show proof of their solution's value to customers - These "proof points' are the M1 of Metrics - They are business outcomes your solution has delivered to your existing customers.

Sellers need to understand the prospect's business outcomes that they are trying to improve - These are the M2's of Metrics, the outcomes your customer cares about improving. They are not only what they are, but how much value your solution provides and who within the customer's organization cares.

A Champion needs to own the Metrics (M1 and M2) - They need to be able to articulate one or two proof points (M1's) to the Economic buyer, and they need to explain the level of improvement of the M2's confidently.

ECONOMIC BUYER

The Economic Buyer is the person
with the overall authority in the
buying decision.

An Economic Buyer is usually one person within an organization who is the overall authority in which the budget for your project rolls up to, however, occasionally, the Economic Buyer can consist of more than one person and, in some instances, is a committee of people.

Identifying the Economic Buyer

The term and definition of 'Economic Buyer' is a sales terminology. You will never find anyone who introduces themselves as the Economic Buyer, therefore, knowing how to identify them is key.

Identification isn't Easy

The Economic Buyer is frequently confused. The cause for this confusion is usually that the Seller has either under-qualified or over-qualified who the Economic Buyer is. That may sound confusing, and it is! Let me break it down:

Under-Qualifying the Economic Buyer - The Budget Holder Mistake:

The most common mistake Sellers make with the Economic Buyer is to under-qualify them, and subsequently halt their investigation once they find a person who says they own the budget.

The person who owns the Budget is the 'Budget Holder'. Just like Economic Buyer, 'Budget Holder' isn't an official title, and customers will rarely pro-actively inform Sellers of who and how their budgeting system works. So, there is not only complexity over the roles of people aligned to budgets but it is also a complicated and confidential system. This is one of the reasons why I recommend not making the budgetary situation a main part of your qualifying criteria.

Another reason why we don't advise the budget being a qualifier of an Economic Buyer is because being a Budget Holder rarely means that you are the Economic Buyer. In fact, much to the contrary, Budget Holders by definition are work-ing to explicit budgets that are aligned to specific departments and projects. Whereas, the criteria of an Economic Buyer is that they have access to discretionary funds and, in many cases, they have the power to shift existing budgets and to obtain new funds. They need this flexibility because they are often empowered to be able to impact major change within their or-ganization.

Over-Qualifying the Economic Buyer - The 'CEO' Mistake:

The other mistake Sellers make when qualifying who the Economic Buyer is, is that they over-qualify and end up nomi-nating someone who is too senior and / or distant from the De-cision Process, for example, the CEO.

Similar to the under-qualifying mistake, this mistake comes from not investigating thoroughly enough. It also comes from not applying intuition to the definition of an Economic Buyer and taking it too literally as the CEO will always have access to discretionary funds and have the power to veto, but they are rarely the Economic Buyer.

Qualifying Criteria

As the misunderstanding about the identity of the Economic Buyer is so common, you should look at a broader criterion such as:

- They have veto power to push the project forward or to stop it regardless of other stakeholders' positions such as your Champion/Counter Champion
- Their focus is in line with the strategic objectives of the organization. You are likely to be able to read about their role or initiatives in the annual report
- They have access to discretionary funds that aren't budgeted
- They are likely to have profit and loss responsibility
- They will sign your contract or be a part of the approval process leading to a signature

Getting Engaged With the Economic Buyer

The success of your deal hinges highly on how well you are able to engage with the Economic Buyer. It is often not an easy process and requires skill, patience, and perseverance.

Consideration should be taken for how and when you engage with the Economic Buyer. This chapter covers the considerations and some strategies to support them.

Your Champion and the Economic Buyer

Your Champion will play a critical role in your process of identifying and engaging with the Economic Buyer.

For this section, we will assume that your Champion is fully qualified as having power and influence, which will be crucial in their role of engaging you with the Economic Buyer.

Your Champion should help you identify your Economic Buyer early on in the sales cycle. You should raise the importance of engagement with the Economic Buyer often to your Champion. It is not acceptable for them to keep you at arm's length as it will seriously impact your ability to make progress on your deal.

Your Champion's role isn't just limited to identification and engagement with the Economic Buyer but they also play an advisory role. The Economic Buyer is likely to be a senior executive and your Champion should coach you on how to work with the Economic Buyer. Questions to ask your Champion:

- How do they like to be engaged? E.g. Phone? Email? Letter?
- What do they care about? E.g. Making Money? Saving Money? Reducing Risk?
- What are some things that you know they like?
- What are some things that you know they dislike?

Context here is important. Get your Champion to open up about notable engagements they have seen the Economic Buyer have in the past. What kinds of approaches did the Economic Buyer like and dislike? Build your approach to suit the Economic Buyer's style and preference.

If your Champion Cannot or Won't Introduce You to the Economic Buyer

On occasion, you will not be able to get an introduction to the Economic Buyer from your Champion. There are a number of reasons that this may occur from the organization having a strict engagement policy, through to your Champion genuinely protecting you in knowledge that the Economic Buyer will be unhappy by your engagement.

In these circumstances, Sellers need to evaluate the circumstances fully. We know that Champions often keep Sellers away from Economic Buyers based on their own perception of whether it will help the deal, but Champions don't necessarily know better than Sellers. One thing is for certain, taking the Champion's guidance to not engage with the Economic Buyer at face value and without investigating further is a mistake and it is one that average Sellers make all the time.

In the situation where a Champion is keeping you away from the Economic Buyer, it is important that you inform your Champion about why they should introduce you. You should have two goals in this process: the first is to explain to your Champion the benefit of introducing you. Explain that it is literally your job to talk to people like the Economic Buyer to support your Champion in their work to buy your solution. The second goal is to train your Champion to talk in the language of the Economic Buyer. They may not be aware that the reasons why they want to buy your solution will be different to that of the Economic Buyer. This is covered in the section below called *Talk the Economic Buyer's Language.*

Other Ways to Engage with the Economic Buyer

Your Champion isn't your only route to your Economic Buyer, and regardless of whether they are willing to introduce you or not, you should always be working on your own direct strategy to engage with the Economic Buyer. Below are a couple of tactics you can deploy:

Going Direct

An often-missed route to the Economic Buyer is to go directly to them. Sellers often overlook this route for fear of upsetting their Champion or for looking disconnected if you are the one to introduce yourself. Whilst it is, of course, better to be introduced to the Economic Buyer, introducing yourself is vastly better than not being in contact at all.

A fear Sellers often have if they have been blocked by their Champion from engaging with the Economic Buyer is that the Champion will be upset if they engage directly. John Kaplan at Force Management has an ace way of circumnavigating this issue and that is to write what he calls 'The Champion Letter'. This is a letter written to the Economic Buyer that introduces yourself and your solution whilst, at the same time, praising your Champion for what an outstanding job they are doing on the project. You can even call out all of the value they have helped you to uncover. It is quite hard for a Champion to be angry at you when you've effectively just been praising them to someone senior within their organization.

Using a Senior Executive to Engage

Aligning your senior executive team with their peers within the customer's organization is good practice. One of the secrets to the success of organizations like Salesforce.com is their ability to engage senior executives on a consistent basis.

However, Sellers frequently wait too long to begin this process and all too often they only ask their senior execs to engage when they feel like they are on the back foot. Elite Sellers engage their senior execs at the earliest point, which can even be before the first meeting.

For example, imagine you have just landed a meeting with your number one prospective customer within your territory. You are excited and begin planning for the first meeting. In your research, you uncover an article written by their Chief Digital Officer talking about an initiative that your solution will support. You ask one of your senior execs to reach out to the CDO and mention that she has heard that her team is meeting with the CDO's team. She also references the article and how she feels your solution can provide value to help her with her initiative. The message doesn't contain any ask, it simply just introduces your senior exec and positions her executive support on the project. It is often good to close with a promise to update the CDO following the meeting on how you heard it went, which leaves the door open for a follow-up.

As this deal progresses, everything could be going smoothly, but if an obstacle comes up, your senior exec already has the line of communication open and can engage in a manner that isn't cold.

The strategy of engaging your senior executives should be followed by all executives you uncover in your deal. You should aim to align them to similarly ranked executives, for instance, C-Level to C-Level or VP to VP.

You should always engage your senior execs with your Economic Buyer regardless of how closely you are engaged with them.

Always be Ready to Engage With the Economic Buyer

It is a sad fact that the majority of selling within our industry leaves a lot to be desired. Buyers have come to expect that Sellers will engage with them without having done any research and are seemingly uninterested in learning about their business. Buyers expect Sellers to rush straight into pitching their solution and, therefore, Sellers generally approach new engagements already on the back foot.

For this reason, first impressions matter, and it is critical that you are prepared for a first interaction with the Economic Buyer that could happen at any time.

We have all had those corridor conversations and instances where a senior exec 'pops into' a meeting. You should be prepared for that.

Once Engaged With the Economic Buyer

This is potentially one of the most critical moments of your deal. Metaphorically speaking, if you get this right, you will have put yourself on pole position for the race ahead. If you get it wrong, you'll be starting in last place with a ton of catching up to do to have any chance of being at the front.

You need to impress upon the Economic Buyer that you are someone that can bring value to them. This starts with talking in their language.

Talk in the Language of the Economic Buyer

"You get delegated to who you sound like."

In your first interaction with the Economic Buyer, they are going to be trying to gauge what kind of a Seller you are. Make no mistake about it, they will have vast experience of working with Sellers—both good and bad—and the chances are they will make their mind up about you in minutes, if not seconds. Therefore, it is crucial that you make the right first impression.

The best way to make the right first impression is by talking in the language of the Economic Buyer, and to do this, you need to have a good understanding of their business objectives. Uncovering these should be part of your research and discovery process, and by the time you meet the Economic Buyer, you should have a good understanding of them.

Practice and Prepare: Elite Sellers must always be ready for surprise engagements with senior executives. Imagine that you are traveling in an elevator to a meeting room with your Champion on a current deal that you are working on. A C-Level person asks you what you are meeting about… what will you say? Are you ready to describe the value of your solution at a moment's notice to any kind of stakeholder? If your answer is no, then this should be a Practice and Preparation Point for you.

From your research and discovery, you will have a good understanding of what the Economic Buyer's current business objectives, pains, and goals are, and you should use these to lead the conversation.

Your objective for your first interaction with the Economic Buyer is simply to get them to see that your partnership can help them reach their business objectives more quickly, or more economically than their current path.

First Interaction Guidance

Behave like a Consultant, not a Seller: This is easier said than done. The chances are, you have been waiting for the opportunity to engage with the Economic Buyer for a while and you don't want to miss your chance to talk about how great your solution is. Hold that urge! Be consultative and don't talk about your solution. Talk about the business objectives and outcomes they are trying to achieve.

Aim to Win Credibility Early: Give industry examples to illustrate your points whilst also demonstrating your knowledge of their industry.

There are two rich sources of information you can use to show your knowledge of their industry.

The first is via reference points from your existing customers:

- What have you helped them solve?
- What results did they see?
- Which mutual connections do you have?
- Who can you introduce them to?

The second is by referring to industry reports and analysis. Even better if you can highlight some industry benchmarks and standards and show how they compare.

Ask Questions: By asking questions, you will not only uncover useful information but you will also separate yourself from the majority of Sellers who use this opportunity to pitch.

Killer-Question:

> *"Champion and I have built some Metrics which we think will measure the success of our solution, but before I show you ours, I'd love to get an idea from you of what you think would be a great indicator of this solution being a success for you?"*

The answer to this question is likely to give you a perception of their goal for your solution. This will help you to strengthen your articulation of your proposition by aligning to it accordingly.

Close Strong: Finish your first interaction by summarizing what you heard on the call from the Economic Buyer and how it relates to the engagement so far. There are likely to be some action points from the call, so re-articulate them and allocate them to owners.

Finally, be bold with any asks you have. It could be something that has come up on the call, or a request for the Economic Buyer to ask another stakeholder to engage in evaluating your solution. Or if none of these things are obvious, then be sure to ask the following Killer-Question:

Killer-Question:

> *"From our conversation today, it seems as though we can really help you solve your objectives.*

> *With your sponsorship, I think we could find more areas of value across the organization. Would you be willing to sponsor the project?"*

Follow-Up: After the first interaction, follow-up by writing an email to the Economic Buyer and copying in your Champion.

The email should exist to serve the Economic Buyer, not the Seller. Therefore, it must include value for the Economic Buyer to balance the asks you will make.

Include evidence that supports any discussion points, such as the business case, or any industry reports in which you referred to.

Summarize the call within the email and ensure any action points are confirmed and the next steps are clearly articulated and allocated to owners.

Hunt the Negatives with the Economic Buyer

Economic Buyers usually have a wealth of experience when it comes to buying solutions. They are likely to have some preconceptions around your solution and offering that need to be uncovered and tackled head-on. Do not shy away from tackling these negatives at the earliest opportunity. Leaving them means they are likely to fester and rise up later in your deal, potentially ruining it.

Don't Expect Them to Get it at First

Economic Buyers, by nature, are dealing with multiple initiatives, and as a result, a number of solutions will cross their desk for them to evaluate. Whereas your Champion may be at the coal face and your solution will instantly make sense, Economic Buyers have a much broader view and are less likely to instantly understand your solution.

In a recent example of this, I was participating in our first meeting with an Economic Buyer of one of the world's biggest banks. The meeting was attended by the top Seller in my team who had recently closed a deal with a subsidiary of the bank and the COO and Co-Founder of the company we worked for. Both the COO and the Seller gave what I noted in my notebook to be *'the best pitch I have ever seen'* of our company. The Economic Buyer responded by asking us how we were different to an entirely different solution that I can only assume he was also evaluating. Fortunately, the Seller was able to distinguish the differences in a polite and articulate manner to correct the Economic Buyer's thinking.

The key thing you should take from this section is just how important it will be for you to engage your solution to the Economic Buyer, as if the best Seller and a co-founder didn't explain the solution in a manner where the Economic Buyer understood, what chance will your Champion have of doing so when you are not around?

How Economic Buyers Make Decisions

We have already established via the qualification criteria of an Economic Buyer that they are focused on the bigger strategic objectives of their organization and that if you want to win credibility with the Economic Buyer, this is where you should focus your conversation.

Economic Buyers do not care about the number of integrations, bells, or whistles that your solution has. What they care about is how much it is going to impact their top or bottom line. It is as simple as that.

If you want to make an impact on the Economic Buyer and for them to remember your solution, you need to ensure it aligns directly with an initiative, goal, or problem that the Economic Buyer is likely to care about. The fastest way to get an Economic Buyer to forget your solution is to talk about its bells and whistles.

When Economic Buyers make decisions, they focus on three Cs:

1. **Cost** - How much will it cost?

2. **Completion** - How long until we can realize the value?

3. **Confidence** - How confident is everyone around your solution?

Let's go a little deeper into each section:

1. Cost - Economic Buyers are not just thinking about the bottom line cost of your solution to their business, they will be evaluating the full business which includes the cost of resources to implement and maintain the solution as well as the potential opportunity cost of prioritizing your solution over others.

2. Completion - The Economic Buyer will be considering the time to value your solution and how that aligns against the other initiatives, strategies, and goals. It is important to keep in mind that an Economic Buyer is most likely looking at results at a quarterly and annual level, and therefore, it is important you do too. Remember that not all organizations follow the same financial years.

3. Confidence - How confident are the buying team around your solution? The Economic Buyer is likely to test all stakeholders, and in particular, your Champion. With this in mind, it is important that you educate your Champion as much as you can for this encounter.

Economic Buyers are likely to have context (and scars) from previous investments that may make them more astute and wary of investments into new solutions. They may also have connections at the executive level to the organizations you have put forward as references, so be sure to check their network where you can, and if you do find a mutual connection who can act as a reference, be sure to be proactive with that opportunity.

You should focus your messaging to the Economic Buyer on the above three areas even if they don't ask about them. It'll hone the conversation to the matters they care about and help to streamline your deal.

Economic Buyer and Go-Live Plan

Introducing the Economic Buyer to the Go-Live Plan opens their exposure to the deal stages that you have consensus from your Champion with as well as the time frames. The Economic Buyer is likely to call out any discrepancies or disagreements he/she has with the data and it is advised to encourage this process as you want to obtain a consensus with the Economic Buyer.

Showing the Go-Live Plan to the Economic Buyer is useful for Sellers to obtain further confirmation of the Decision and Paper Processes, in particular, who signs and whether there are any stages that have been missed such as additional layers of authority where approval is required.

Economic Buyer and Procurement

Procurement are seldom the Economic Buyer. They may be acting on behalf of the Economic Buyer, which is basically a Procurement's job.

In enterprise sales, it is common for deals to have to run the gauntlet with Procurement, but it doesn't have to be that way. Unlike Champions who generally will guide you on how to engage with Procurement, Economic Buyers can help you circumnavigate Procurement entirely.

Put simply, if you have uncovered enough value for your Economic Buyer and attached what you do to their most important business objectives, then the Economic Buyer could help you skip Procurement all together.

Where circumnavigation isn't possible, your Economic Buyer can chaperone you through Procurement, radically increasing the speed of the process and potentially keeping your margins intact.

Economic Buyer and Your Sales Process

The Economic Buyer is likely to be present throughout your deal cycle, although in the early stages you may not feel their presence, if the deal is qualified, then the Economic Buyer should be aware of the project.

Early-Stages:

Opinions on the importance of early engagement with the Economic Buyer vary. Some will advise you to engage with the Economic Buyer as early and often as possible, whilst others will advise you to delay engagement in the early stages while you build an understanding of where you can provide value and how it relates to the organization's challenges.

My view is that both perspectives have merit and it comes down to the Seller to make a call as to when the right time to engage is, however, Sellers should always look to make an introduction of themselves as soon as they have firmly identified who the Economic Buyer is.

This introduction doesn't have to be a big event, nor does it call for any action from the Economic Buyer. It can simply be an email from the Seller introducing themselves and high-level details of the project they are working on and with whom. In most cases, you will get a reply thanking you for the introduction and usually a note that says something like "I am looking forward to seeing how the opportunity progresses". You could also get a note that highlights that the project isn't a priority, or that it is. Either way, there is very little downside to making this introduction at the earliest possibility.

In most deals, the Economic Buyer won't be engaged from the start and the Seller will have to be proactive to get them engaged. Although, it isn't impossible that the Economic Buyer can be engaged from the start, especially if the problem you are solving is a big one or you have been introduced to the organization at an executive level. In these instances, it is even more important that you have done the research detailed in the previous section.

If the Economic Buyer isn't engaged in the early stages, then it is important that the Seller works on uncovering who they are, what the political landscape surrounding them is, as well as how they are impacted by any challenges you have uncovered.

In the early stages, you will be working hard to uncover what the Decision Criteria and Process is likely to be. The Economic Buyer is likely to play a part in both the Decision Process and Criteria, and understanding the dynamics of their involvement will be useful to building your understanding of those stages of MEDDICC as well as the role the Economic Buyer will play in your deal.

Early Consensus:

In the early stages, you want to obtain a consensus on who the Economic Buyer is, and how they are involved in the deal, as well as how they will be involved going forward.

Specifically, you want to understand how the Pain you have uncovered impacts their business objectives.

An Economic Buyer can often provide a fresh perspective on your deal that a Champion can't give you.

Mid-Stages:

In the mid-stages of your deal, you need to have direct engagement with the Economic Buyer.

At this point, you need to have confirmation from the Economic Buyer that they see the full value of your solution. This should be achieved by illustrating how strongly your solution aligns with the Decision Criteria and displays the Metrics that underpin the value.

Ideally, you will have reached a consensus with your Champion and the Economic Buyer on the value you provide prior to finalizing the scope and subsequently the final costs of your solution. Giving pricing prior to having consensus on the value could lead to a perception that your solution doesn't represent value for money, AKA you are expensive.

If you have affirmation of your value from the Economic Buyer, then you should progress to trying to obtain the final buy-in from your Economic Buyer on your solution.

If delivered correctly, your final proposal should illustrate value underpinned by the Metrics you will use together to measure the success of the solution once live. The proposal should represent a return on investment so strong that proceeding forward with your solution seems like an obvious decision.

Mid Consensus:

In the mid-stages, you will be looking for multiple levels of consensus from the Economic Buyer. Starting with how your solution solves her business objectives and later shifting to how your solution matches their Decision Criteria. Finally, the Economic Buyer should agree a consensus with the value you illustrate within their business case.

Late-Stages:

As you enter into the late stages of your deal, you are looking for commitment from the Economic Buyer that you are their vendor of choice and they support your business case.

The Economic Buyer can play a highly useful role around the Paper Process as their influence can help you streamline the process and fly through stages with the momentum their sponsorship creates.

Late Consensus:

The Go-Live Plan provides a great tool for obtaining late-stage consensus as you can confirm the stages with the Economic Buyer and obtain the support to complete the stages still ahead of you.

Summary Snapshot of in the sales process:

- Early: How much will you help me? Do I believe you?
- Mid: How does this value compare to others?

- Late: Have you proven that this value is available?

Economic Buyer after you've won the deal

Once your deal is closed, the Economic Buyer is unlikely to have any further hands-on activity with your solution.

Elite Sellers know that keeping the Economic Buyer informed on the progress of the implementation of the solution will reap rewards later on for the Seller, when they want to re-engage in a renewal or upsell conversation. Not forgetting the likelihood that the Economic Buyer could become an invaluable reference for your future deals if you deliver on your promises to them.

Summary of Economic Buyer

I will close this chapter the same way I opened it:

The Economic Buyer can say "No" when other people say "Yes" and "Yes when other people say "No".

Engagement with the Economic Buyer is important but equally as important is how we engage with them.

If you follow the advice throughout this book, then your engagements with Economic Buyers will be focused on value and they will see you as a trusted advisor, putting you in the fast lane to getting deals done with their sponsorship.

A word from Jack on Economic Buyer

Sales leaders should attend Economic Buyer meetings - It's the Seller and her Champion's show. Still, a leader should attend to provide support to the Seller. Also, the leader has the power to make decisions in that meeting that the Seller may not have.

Why did you take this meeting? - Instead of launching into a presentation after the intros, the attending sales leader should ask the Economic Buyer why they took the meeting. This will provide valuable insight into how the discussion should proceed.

Follow up - Always ask the Economic Buyer for their contact information. If you've had a good meeting, they will want to connect with you. If not, they will defer. An exception to this is if they defer to the Champion. This is a good sign that they support your Champion.

Either way, the sales leader should always create their own communication line with the Economic Buyer.

DECISION CRITERIA

The Decision Criteria is the sets of principles, guidelines, and requirements that an organization uses to make a decision.

A good way to visualize the Decision Criteria is to picture a checklist of requirements that your customer is looking for you to satisfy. They are usually more than just technical requirements and are likely to include business-based and holistic criteria too.

The Decision Criteria is often represented by MEDDICC definitions as being something that exists within your customer's Decision Process in which they are closely evaluating your solution. The reality is that the Decision Criteria is a selling term and customers will rarely have one completely worked out.

Instead, it is more common that your main stakeholders will have an informal consensus between themselves of the criteria the solution will need to meet.

There are scenarios where it is more likely that the customer has a more formal Decision Criteria such as if they are running a RFP or they are a more formal organization such as government or public-sector organization.

However, regardless of whether the Decision Criteria has been formalized or not, your customer will expect you to influence their Decision Criteria with your own perspectives and thought leadership.

It is, therefore, critical that you get your hands wrapped around the Decision Criteria as early as possible.

Establishing the Status of the Decision Criteria

The first step of this is to understand whether a formal Decision Criteria exists. If you have been approached and invited to participate in an evaluation, then it is more likely that there will be a Decision Criteria than if you have drummed up the interest yourself.

If Your Customer Has Established a Decision Criteria

Your customer is likely to be basing their Decision Criteria upon a number of considerations. This could be from the gold standard analyst like Gartner and Forrester, through to online review sites such as G2Crowd, third-party consultancies, and agencies, or even other solution providers they work with as well as your Competition.

It is an important task to uncover what sources are influencing the Decision Criteria as understanding this will help you to obtain context as to where the criteria came from and will help set you up to compliment it or counter it as need be.

I once worked with a Seller who had a deal where the Decision Criteria specified that the solution was hosted on servers inside of the European Union. This was a valuable deal, which had the potential to be the biggest in the company's history. Feeling the gravity of losing the deal, the Seller went like a bull in a china shop to his CTO asking him to set up servers in Europe. It was something that was on the roadmap, so the CTO said he would investigate, but checked in with the Seller's manager first, who wasn't aware of the request. The manager told the CTO to pause while he investigated further and found out from the customer that the basis of their requirement came from an analyst who had incorrectly reported on the GDPR legislation. Subsequently, there was no need for European servers and the deal pressed on ahead.

As always, when it comes to uncovering information from your customer, the best method to do this is via discovery. Simple questions like the one below and those detailed within the discovery section will help you to unlock the context of how the customer has established their Decision Criteria:

> *"You suggested that having servers within Europe was part of your Decision Criteria, what makes that an important part of the specification?"*

"The Analyst at ABC stated that we need to have servers hosted within the European Union to be GDPR compliant."

You now know, as per the earlier example, that part of the Decision Criteria is incorrect as well as knowing they follow the advice of a certain analyst when building their Decision Criteria. Is there anything else that the same analyst is likely to have influenced in the Decision Criteria? You could probably find out just by asking.

Once you have established the existing Decision Criteria, you need to assess whether you feel it is favorable to your solution and whether you stand a good chance of winning against it. If the Decision Criteria is clearly unfavorable to your solution, then you have to make the decision as to whether you feel as though you can influence it to shift in favor of your solution or whether you should qualify out.

If There is No Clearly Established Decision Criteria

This may seem like the optimum scenario as it means you have a blank canvas to work with, but it can also be a major red flag either because your customer hasn't thought enough about what should be considered when buying your solution or because they are immature buyers. Both scenarios are bad news for you.

If you feel as though the aforementioned reasons are why there is no Decision Criteria, then just as when the Decision Criteria is unfavorable to you, you have to decide whether you think you can influence the Decision Criteria to be favorable to you or whether you should qualify out.

If you choose to try and influence the criteria, it is important that you have strong consensus from multiple stakeholders that they are motivated to explore a full evaluation of your solution.

In all instances, Sellers need to work on influencing the Decision Criteria, but as the Decision Criteria breaks down into three different parts, it is important that we first learn about these parts before we talk about influencing them.

The Three Types of Decision Criteria

You can define the Decision Criteria into three different types:

1. **Technical** - Does your solution technically meet the requirements to make it feasible for the requirements outlined?

2. **Economic** - Matters relating to how viable your solution is from a perspective of finance, Risk, and efficiency.

3. **Relationship** - How closely do the values and direction of the two organizations align?

The importance of each type will depend on which stakeholder you are talking to. For instance, the Economic Buyer will normally rely on his/her teams to establish that your solution passes the technical criteria, but they themselves are likely to be interested in the business criteria.

Let's take a look at how each type breaks down:

Technical Decision Criteria

The Technical Decision Criteria ties the technical requirements of the solution together with your solution's capabilities.

Primarily, your customer will be looking to you to confirm that your solution can deliver upon the use-cases that have been set out for your solution to solve. Generally, the criteria to answer this will lie in your solution's functionality but it doesn't mean that the technical criteria will be limited to just your functionality. In fact, it is often the lack of holistic technical requirements that sink deals.

Let's take a look at what the Holistic technical criteria is likely to be:

Infrastructure - Does your solution match up to the standards the customer requires of their infrastructure, both from a performance and security perspective?

Integrations - Does your solution integrate with your customer's existing technology stack and does the customer feel confident that you will be able to integrate with future solutions they invest in?

Ease of Use - Does the customer feel confident that your solution is intuitive and usable?

The technical criteria are different from the business and partner criteria for two reasons. The first is that it is generally more important as the customer may take a chance on you if you don't meet the business or partner criteria, but if you don't pass the technical criteria, they are unlikely to take a Risk. Secondly, whereas the business and partner criteria can be very fluid based on the feelings of the customer, the technical criteria is far more binary, often coming down to yes or no of whether you can feasibly support the requirements.

Technical Decision Criteria and RFPs

It is often the technical criteria that make up the majority of the contents of a RFP and if you find yourself involved in a Blind RFP (a process where your organization had no previous engagement), it is important that you rapidly establish whether the RFP has been influenced by another party such as a competitor.

Economic Decision Criteria

The Economic Decision Criteria is often referred to as the 'Financial Criteria'. I prefer to refer to it as the Economic Decision Criteria as I believe it is the economics that enterprise organizations are interested in and when you label the criteria as 'financial', far too many Sellers just think of cost instead of the overall economics which is where they are better off focusing.

Another reason why I like to refer to this section as the Economic Decision Criteria is that the components usually considered within this section matter most to the Economic Buyer. If you want to make this point crystal clear, you could even call this section the Economic Buyer Decision Criteria.

The fundamental factor of the economics is having a rock-solid business case. The crucial component in any business case is the Return on Investment (ROI). Most organizations will have a required ROI ratio which means that for every $ they spend, they will want to get a multiple amount back. My experience is that if you simply ask the customer what their required ratio is, they are likely to tell you. I have seen ratios as low as 1.5x right up to 10x requirements.

There are likely to be other economic criteria. Some examples of which are:

Risks - How does your solution help the organization to reduce or mitigate any Risks they are facing?

Time - What is the amount of time that is associated with your solution? Both from a time to value perspective and in terms of outright time required to implement and maintain it.

Opportunity Cost - What is the value of your solution versus other opportunities the customer is considering and what will be the cost of prioritizing your solution over them?

Commercial terms - As crazy as it often seems, I have seen organizations pass on solution providers who weren't able to be flexible on commercial terms as seemingly trivial as invoice payment terms.

Relationship Decision Criteria

The Relationship Decision Criteria relates to how closely your organization aligns with the customer's. There are many elements that contribute towards the relationship of two organizations and they tend to be more holistic than formal.

Here are a few elements that are likely to be consistent:

Executive Alignment/Sponsorship - Do the interests and values of the organization's executives align? Does your customer feel as though they have executive-level support? I have seen executive engagement turn the tide of deals before.

Industry and Direction - Do the directions of the organizations align? For instance, if your customer is a retailer, are you able to demonstrate that you are actively moving in the direction to do more in retail?

Reputation - What is your reputation in the eyes of your customer? Do third-party partners recommend you? Are online reviews favorable? Have you connected the customer with relevant references?

Open and Collaborative - Does the customer find you and your team open and collaborative to work with? Can they foresee themselves having a good working relationship with you?

Fair and Reasonable - Have you shown yourself to be fair and reasonable? This could relate to commercial or legal terms, or perhaps you have waived some initial costs as a sign of good faith.

Skin in the Game - Do you have skin in the game? Are you sharing the Risk with the customer?

The weight of the Relationship Decision Criteria doesn't often tend to be evaluated very closely until both the Technical and Economic Decision Criteria have been evaluated. Once they are passed, then the customer will tend to pay closer attention to the Relationship-related elements.

Influencing the Decision Criteria

Influencing the Decision Criteria is where Elite Sellers really come into their own. They know that to effectively influence the Decision Criteria, they have to be at their best as the influencing process requires the pinnacle of expertise that can only come from a thorough discovery process and a strong understanding of both the customer's industry and how their solution suits it.

It all starts with discovery. Understanding deeply what the Pains and goals of the organization are. Being able to go deep and uncover a full understanding of the pain and then being able to link that pain to a solution you can provide that is illustrated by clear use-cases and then traced back to capabilities that only your solution can provide. This is the most direct way to influence the Decision Criteria and if you find yourself amongst the Elite who regularly do this, then make sure you put the cherry on top by linking the value of this part of your solution into Metrics.

If you have engaged with the customer early in the evaluation, or perhaps you sparked their interest, then there is a good chance that you will have a priceless opportunity to define the Decision Criteria. If you sense that your customer is going to progress forward by formalizing their Decision Criteria, then be sure to offer your services in helping them define it. In an ideal world, they will want you to build the entirety of the specification, but it is more likely that you will get a chance to influence it by sending over some things that you think should be requirements. Even in the worst-case scenario where the customer declines your input, it is still worth sending over some documentation that could assist them in building the specification as I can guarantee you nobody will enjoy building the specification, and if there is a ready-made one sat in their inbox, there is a good chance they will at least look at it.

Working with Practical Decision Criteria

Often, customers will surface their Decision Criteria into a practical exercise for the solution provider to work with such as a RFP, or something more mutually hands-on like a Canned Demo, a Proof of Concept, or a Pilot. These are usually set with a requirement to follow a set specification which usually relates closely to the Decision Criteria.

In the first instance when a customer invites you to participate in a practical exercise, it is important that you qualify firmly what the success criteria is of the exercise and what the outcome will be of prevailing success from it. If the customer is unclear on what the success criteria will be, then it is ok for you to help them specify it as this is effectively you influencing the Decision Criteria for the exercise.

Further still, you should seek clarity on what you will gain following a successful outcome of any practical exercise. Without this clarity, you should hold your ground firmly and not invest your resources until you know what is in it for you.

Far too often, Sellers mistake engagement from customers as being progress so they sit spinning their wheels, throwing their solution experts at their opportunities to try and prove and re-prove that they meet the Decision Criteria. Meanwhile, their Competition is in the background pulling strings to influence it to favor their solution.

If You Don't Influence the Decision Criteria, Your Competition Will

Regardless of how established you think your customer is with their Decision Criteria, your Competition will always be actively trying to influence it to suit their strengths and unique selling points. If you are not careful, your Competition could be influential in defining the Decision Criteria which puts your solution immediately on the back foot.

Keep in mind that your Competition isn't just limited to your rivals but can also be an initiative to build internally or other projects and priorities competing for the same resources. Keep this in mind when considering how broad the Decision Criteria could be. It could also be that your solution falls inside of a wider initiative of which many types of solutions are being considered. Getting these facts out in the open is critical for your understanding of where you stand.

Turn Vague Into Visible: Articulation and Awareness

In the instance where you find yourself influencing the Decision Criteria, it is important that you do what you can to make it clear to your customer what the Decision Criteria are so that they can clearly articulate them to other people in the organization to raise awareness for them.

Far too often, Sellers uncover unique Decision Criteria that only they can solve and don't do a good enough job of circulating the information around the customer's organization. This results in the customer assuming that either it isn't a particularly unique differentiation, or even worse, that your competitors have it too.

Link the Decision Criteria to the Metrics

An Elite MEDDICC move is to link the Decision Criteria to Metrics, especially if you have added a unique differentiator to the Decision Criteria that you can then underpin with a Metric.

For instance, if you uncover that your customer could benefit from your unique functionality of having Chinese languages within their interface, you would not only add that as a Decision Criteria but also break it down into a Metric to highlight just how much more productive the team in China will be by having this functionality. If you can quantify this improvement in productivity then you will have successfully influenced the Decision Criteria with a trap for your competition that is underpinned by a Metric.

Taking Score

Within this chapter, we have talked at length about uncovering and influencing the Decision Criteria but of equal importance is being able to understand how your customer is scoring you against their Decision Criteria.

A good technique to do this is to talk through the Decision Criteria you are aware of with your customer and ask them to give feedback about how you are scoring against each part.

It is worth asking if there are any areas where the customer has concern or where they think you fall short. It is much better to have these issues out in the open so you can work on solving them rather than leaving them festering in your customer's head. Also, these issues could be the results of traps set by your competition that you haven't set off yet.

Building a Business Case

As mentioned earlier in this chapter, a major component of the Economic Decision Criteria is the Business Case.

Your business case should include the following sections and considerations:

Executive Summary

The executive summary should illustrate the reasoning for initiating the implementation of your solution.

It should discuss the current state and Pain that is felt because of it. It should point to the future Utopian state that your solution will provide and how your solution is the only one that delivers enough of the Decision Criteria to deliver upon the desired future state.

It should highlight the headline numbers from your business case, for instance, if your solution will drive increases in revenue and that is the primary value driver, you should call it out front and center.

The Numbers Part

This is the main part of your business case. The calculations should be based on numbers that the customers have either given you directly of confirmed are accurate if obtained from an alternative source. Often, you will be able to find useful financial data within the organization's annual report and other documentation that is publicly available.

The Two Highest Priorities For Your Business Case:

Easy to Read - Your business case will be passed around your customer's business, including to people you haven't met. For this reason, the business case needs to be written in a language everyone can understand. No buzzwords or terminology that isn't widely understood.

Credibility - The impact of your business case hinges almost entirely on how credible the reader believes it is. For this reason, the data has to be accurate and relevant. Your Champion will be crucial in helping you compile and confirm the legitimacy of the business case data.

The Champion Owned Business Case

In some instances, the Champion themselves will take ownership of the business case, This is generally a positive thing as the credibility of the document will be much higher. However, it is important that you keep in touch with the contents and that the parts of value that are unique to your solution are highlighted. You do not want to build a business case only for your Competition to benefit!

Proof and Test

Often, Sellers are working against such tight time constraints to send over the business case that they don't put enough effort in the final and yet most important stage—the proofing and testing stage.

Ensuring your document is proofed for grammatical, spelling, and formatting errors is an obvious stage of proofing that is often skipped. Also, the data itself will need to be checked that it is all accurate and, finally, you will want to check with the people proofing for you that the main messages come across. To do this, ask them to read through it and report back to you what they felt the key messages were. If they do not align with your intention, you have work to do prior to sending your document.

Decision Criteria Document

Including a breakdown of your interpretation of the Decision Criteria is an elite move, especially if you can make it seem as though you are simply articulating what you have heard. When this is done right, you have a genuine chance of locking in your interpretation of the Decision Criteria to be the official version.

For this reason, it should appear as vanilla and unbiased as possible. You should use generic terms that are not related to you or your solution. While this may seem an underhand move, being underhand is actually counter-productive to the purpose. You need for this document to have full credibility and the only way to do that is to represent the facts in an honest manner. It is likely you will be biased, but that is ok if the bias is backed by data and facts.

Decision Criteria and Procurement

If you have been able to uncover unique parts of the Decision Criteria that only your solution can deliver upon, then it is important to ensure that Procurement is aware of this as it will help you defend your value against your Competition should you need to.

Decision Criteria and Your Sales Process

The Decision Criteria plays an important role throughout the sales process. You are also likely to find that it will adapt and evolve with each stage and keeping a handle on it will be critical to your success.

Early-Stages:

Within your first engagement with your customer, you need to quickly establish what their status is in relation to your solution. Are you the first person to present a solution like yours to them? Or have you been invited to engage in an evaluation that has been meticulously planned by the customer?

Obtaining this understanding early on and establishing the status of the Decision Criteria is crucial.

If your customer has Decision Criteria, then work to understand the details of it and find out the instances that led those Decision Criteria to being created. Understanding this could uncover what their major drivers for the evaluation are as well as potentially uncovering Competition and their strengths.

If your customer doesn't have a Decision Criteria at this stage, then this is your first opportunity to seize and influence it.

Throughout your discovery Process, be sure to look for Pain that can be translated into Decision Criteria.

Within the early stages, you need to be able to positively impact the Decision Criteria towards your strengths, and at the very least, you will want to have insight from your Champion into the Decision Criteria.

Mid-Stages:

By the mid-stages, the Decision Criteria should be clearly formalized by your customer. If it isn't, you should have an active track of work with your Champion to work towards having consensus.

Your Champion should be socializing the Decision Criteria with other stakeholders, including the Economic Buyer.

Once the Decision Criteria is in place, you will want to validate that your solution scores well against the Decision Criteria and that there are no concerns about the feasibility of your solution.

Your Champion should also inform you about how you are shaping up against the Competition at this stage so you can adapt to overcome any shortfalls you have.

As you move towards the later stages of the Decision Process, your Champion will need to be playing strongly in your corner to inform other stakeholders about your solution scores against the Decision Criteria.

Late-Stages:

In the late stages of your deal, the Technical Decision Criteria and how well your solution fits against it is likely to be locked in place. Hopefully, by this point, you will have done enough to ensure your suitability and strengths have been understood by your customer. The only thing you can do at this stage is to work on ensuring the Decision Criteria and how you measure up against it is clearly understood and communicated across all stakeholders.

The Economic and Relationship Decision Criteria could still be open to evaluation and because these Criterion are less binary than the Technical Decision Criteria, it is important that you continue to be pro-active on qualifying your status with each. Asking stakeholders questions like:

"Do the Metrics within the business case resonate with all stakeholders?"

"Do you or your colleagues have any reservations with our team and working with us?"

The answers to questions like these should give a good insight into the status of how you score against Economic and Relationship Decision Criteria.

Summary Snapshot of in the Sales Process:

- Early: Do you have a Decision Criteria? What is it? What has influenced it? How can you influence it?

- Mid: Do all stakeholders know the Decision Criteria and how you uniquely solve against it? How do you score?

- Late: Do you have consensus that you solve the Decision Criteria better than anyone else? If not, what are you doing to solve that?

Summary of Decision Criteria

The Decision Criteria is a critical part of your customer's Decision Process. Whether or not they have a Decision Criteria formalized, you have to be involved. It is imperative that you get your hands wrapped around it to understand, and where possible, influence it.

A word from Jack on Decision Criteria

The Sales Engineer should own the Technical Decision Criteria - Putting the Technical Decision Criteria under the Sales Engineer's custody is best practice. They are the best qualified to understand and own it.

Decision Criteria flushes out a lot of the vagueness in an enterprise deal - The Decision Criteria is a cornerstone to the MEDDICC methodology. When capabilities are tied to outcomes and weighing per category, you have something tangible to discuss with the stakeholders, your Champion, and others in the Decision Process.

Make agreeing to a Decision Criteria with your Champion part of their qualification criteria - If you have a true Champion, they will be happy to collaborate with you to build a bulletproof Decision Criteria.

DECISION PROCESS

The Decision Process is a series of steps that dictates how your customer will make a decision.

Who are the people involved and what processes will those people go through in order to evaluate, select, and purchase your solution?

From the What to the How

The Decision Criteria is the *what* the decision will be based on and the Decision Process is the **how** the decision will be made.

Whereas the Decision Criteria is what will decide whether you become the customer's vendor of choice. It is the Decision Process that will decide whether your deal closes on time or slips.

Uncovering the Decision Process and Progressing Through it

It is your job to uncover the Decision Process as early as possible and then to consistently work on validating each step with every stakeholder you come across.

Once you have established the Decision Process, every input and effort you make should be directed towards passing through the steps of the Decision Process ahead of you. Once you feel you have passed a step, you need to obtain validation that you have done so from your customer.

Rarely Less, Always More!

No matter how you obtain the Decision Process, whether it is clearly articulated to you via a formal document or you have it from a thorough discovery process, it is likely that more parts will be added to it that you are yet to uncover or that don't exist yet. For this reason, you need to stay in discovery mode to hunt down any changes as well as seek confirmation of the process and where you stand against it at every opportunity.

While it is likely that there will be more steps added to the Decision Process, it is rarely the case that you will have to go through fewer steps than what an official or validated version of the Decision Process states. You should always approach any loopholes or shortcuts to the Decision Process with cynicism. Paranoia is your friend, and if something seems too good to be true, it usually is.

There are Two Parts: Validation and Approval

The Decision Process breaks into two parts: the Technical Validation and the Business Approval.

Both parts are linked, but usually run independently of each other with the Technical Validation coming first.

Technical Validation

The Technical Validation is the process your customer goes through to validate your solution's feasibility to solve the requirements set out in the Decision Criteria.

The manner in which your customer runs through this validation will vary. But it will generally always include product demos and sessions between both organization's technical teams. In more formal instances, they may involve a RFP process, a Proof of Concept, or Pilot. The latter of these items may also be part of the process to approve the business objectives of the initiative, which we talk about next.

Business Approval

Once the technical validation has taken place, the business approval process begins.

Note: The business approval process can run in parallel to the technical validation and in instances such as where there is a POC or Pilot, the two can be linked, but it is very unlikely that the business approval process will start ahead of the technical process. This occurring should be treated as a Red Flag for your deal and you should seek an understanding of the technical validation immediately.

The business approval process consists of the steps and stages that you need to pass for the customer to be able to state that they are making a decision to proceed with your solution.

Note: At this stage, the Decision Process starts to morph into the Paper Process which is detailed in the next chapter. The Paper Process forms the P in MEDDPICC, but as you will no doubt have noticed, some organizations implement MEDDICC. This usually means that they are incorporating the Paper Process into the Decision Process.

Doing this can be a logical and practical way to implement MEDDICC and is worth considering if you want to reduce the perception of the number of fields that MEDDICC requires to be learned and maintained.

The advantage to calling out the Paper Process is that it separates a crucial stage of your deal and keeps it prominently in mind.

Within the business approval process, it isn't about just steps and stages but engagement with people too. Understanding the people who need to approve your solution is crucial. You will need to obtain answers to questions like:

- Who needs to approve this deal?
- What is their role?
- Are there any committees or formal boards?
- How long does each person take?
- Who or what can slow this down?
- Who can help me speed it up?

Decision Process and Go-Live Plan

Elite Sellers know that to ace the Decision Process, they need to be able to have visibility of every step: who are the stakeholders involved and what are the dependencies of each step?

Sharing the mapped steps of the Decision Process with your customer on a Go-Live Plan will help to qualify your understanding of the Decision Process.

Always work backwards from the goal. If the goal is to go-live by a certain date then factor in the time it will take to implement the solution and the stages of the Paper Process and work backwards through the stages of the Decision Process with your customer.

Building a Go-Live Plan this way will help you set milestones and uncover dependencies. It will also help to hold your customer accountable for each step's progression.

Never Assume Your Go-Live Plan is Correct

Never assume that just because you have worked through the Decision Process on your Go-Live Plan with your Champion that it is complete.

Your Go-Live Plan is not complete until all of the steps are passed. The Go-Live Plan can (and will) change, often frequently. Keeping track of progress against the Decision Process is key to being able to accurately forecast the deal's close date.

It is imperative that you socialize the Go-Live Plan across all of the stakeholders involved within the Decision Process. Each stakeholder will have different parts in the process and if you rely on the consensus of just one stakeholder, you are going to sleepwalk yourself into a surprise once you realize you only have clarity on one stakeholder's version of the Decision Process.

Work With Your Network and Partners

Remember to ask any third parties who may have experience of working with your customer for details of their experience and any advice they can give you.

I can recall one instance where a casual conversation with a third-party highlighted to me that my customer required vendors to agree a large indemnity in their contracts. The amount was so high that it would take weeks to get to a point where we could satisfy the requirement. Fortunately, as I knew about it earlier than when it would have come up in a normal circumstance, I was able to get ahead of it and solve it. That deal was signed at 10 pm on the last day of the quarter, proving that every second counts!

Influencing the Decision Process

Most parts of the Decision Process are firmly in place as they form the structure of processes in which your customer must satisfy to make any major purchase. Therefore, being able to influence the Decision Process the same way you can influence the Decision Criteria is a challenge.

However, there are some techniques you can use to influence the timing or the Decision Process or to add extra steps to the Decision Process itself:

Influence the Timing

By using a Go-Live Plan and following the advice above, you may be able to influence the customer to start a step earlier due to a later dependency or timing constraint upon another stage.

Add Additional Steps

Add additional steps to the Decision Process where you are confident you will score strongly over your Competition. An example of this would be to encourage your customer to make a reference call to a third-party technology that the Decision Criteria requires you to have an integration with. If this third-party vendor prefers your solution, it can be a strong strategy to add an independent positive reference to your armory.

Measure Progress Against the Decision Process, Not Effort and Engagement

The most common mistake I see when Sellers are evaluating the Decision Process is that they mistake effort and engagement for progress. The Seller's strategy is to throw as much effort as they can at their customers with demos, reference calls, reports, and engagement from their executives and experts in the hope that it shines a positive light on them and keeps the deal moving forward. The bad news is that hope and effort are not strategies.

This is what happens when Sellers are moving forward without a clear direction and MEDDICC and the Decision Process is what will give them that direction.

The Kiss of Death Compliment

Early in my sales career, I had what was at the time a highly embarrassing experience which I now reflect on as one of the most informing of my career.

I was leading a major engagement between Oracle and a multi-billion-dollar global organization. At the time, I thought I was doing a great job. The truth was that I was well and truly out of my depth.

The VP of Sales was ex-BMC and clearly had some doubts about the health of my deal. Of course, I felt he was wrong. I was working pretty much full-time on the deal, there was tons of engagement from the customer. If the deal closed, it would have put me over 200% of my annual target in the one deal alone! The VP asked me to set up a meeting with him and the CIO, who was my Champion.

The meeting took place in one of Oracle's plush meeting rooms. A grandiose room that was plusher than most board rooms. The VP wasted little time in trying to get an understanding of the Decision Criteria and Decision Process from the CIO. It was all very vague, but at the time, I thought that was OK because they must have liked us... why else would they be engaging so much with us?

The VP dug and dug and it soon became apparent that there was a lot more work to be done for this engagement to be considered a solid deal, let alone one closing that financial year.

Sensing the challenges the VP had uncovered, the CIO, my Champion, piped up:

> *"I really must say, Andy has been absolutely first-class for us all throughout this project. He has been extremely professional, and has given us all of the information we've needed at every step."*

I could feel a stupid grin coming over my face. Here was the CIO of a multi-billion-dollar company praising me to the VP of Sales, not just my boss, but my boss's boss's boss. However, my smile didn't last long because, without skipping a single second, the VP replied:

> *"Well, thank you, but here at Oracle we rate our salespeople by what they have sold, and Andy hasn't sold you anything yet."*

Ouch!

Of course, he was absolutely right. A few weeks later, the CIO left the business and a month or so after that, the customer selected Microsoft, a competitor we hadn't even identified was in the mix.

Decision Process and your Sales Process

In your sales process, it is important that you seek to understand information about the Decision Process at the earliest opportunity. It will help you to ascertain how serious the customer is about getting a deal done as well as helping you to accurately forecast it at every step.

Early-Stages:

Understanding early in your deal how your customer makes decisions is going to give you the information you need to set yourself on the right course for success.

If the opportunity is well qualified and the customer is serious about buying a solution, they will be open to your inquests into the Decision Process. If the customer is closed about it or is unable to offer any useful information, this should be classed as a major red flag for the qualification of your deal and you should consider qualifying out.

Within the early stages, you will want to uncover the Technical Decision Process; how will they validate whether a solution is feasible for their needs and who are the stakeholders and departments that are involved within that process?

Mid-Stages:

By the mid-stages, you should have a full understanding of the Decision Process and be keeping your finger tightly on the pulse of it to spot any changes as they happen.

Your Champion should be keeping you up to date at every step and you should both be tracking your progress within the Go-Live Plan. Should anything change, or you fall behind for any reason, your Champion should be working with you to get back on top.

The deal should be moving consistently forward and as you approach the later stage, the Decision Process is likely to switch towards the Business Approval part of the Decision Process.

At this point, your Champion should be preparing you for your engagement with the Legal and Procurement teams, if required.

Late-Stages:

In the late stages of the Decision Process, the Technical Validation should be locked in as should the Business Validation, if it isn't, then it should be close to being so, or you should have a clear and mapped out path to completion.

It is understanding the Decision Process at the late stages that is going to be the difference between your deal closing and slipping.

Summary Snapshot of in the Sales Process:

- Early: How does the customer make a decision?

- Mid: I fully understand how the decision in my deal is going to be made and I am tracking my progress against each step
- Late: Everything is on track against the Decision Process and I am managing the final steps

Summary

Thought leaders within the sales industry frequently talk about the importance of aligning the selling process to how the customer buys, and in my opinion, there is no better way to do that than by aligning everything you do as a Seller with the way in which your customer makes decisions, aka their Decision Process.

If before every activity you undertake on your deal, you ask yourself how it helps you progress against your customer's Decision Process, then you will both align yourself to progress with your customer and your deal.

A word from Jack on Decision Process

Work backward from the compelling event - Define the compelling event with the Champion and then work back to establish the events and milestones you will be executing against hand in hand with your customer.

Orchestrate Throughout - Enterprise-level deals are complicated. You need to orchestrate the Decision Process with the Champion to set up the sequencing of the events. You need to know what other customers have done to make an informed decision and share that with your Champion.

Validate Costs with the Economic Buyer - You should aim to meet with the Economic Buyer before any instance where you are giving a quotation for your solution. Within this meeting, you need to indicate the likely cost and ROI to the Economic Buyer to set their expectations.

PAPER PROCESS

The Paper Process is the steps or actions that lie in place ahead of contracts being agreed and signed.

Generally, most of the Paper Process begins once the Seller has been given a clear indication that they have been selected. Usually, this means that the specifications and commercial elements of the deal have been agreed upon; however, they may still be in play in some instances.

The Paper Process doesn't tend to differ too much regardless of the state of the deal specification or commercials, unless the difference in specification or commercials pushes the deal into a new boundary of approval requirements.

The specification of the Paper Process will vary from customer to customer. However, the endpoint of the process is always the same—for the Seller, it is a signed contract, and for the buyer, it is the approval to release funds for the investment and to sign the Seller's contract.

There is a lot of cross-over between the Paper Process and the Decision Process, and in some variations of MEDDICC, the Paper Process is rolled inside the Paper Process. For this chapter, we will treat the Paper Process as its own individual part.

You Need Your Champion

No Seller can tackle the Paper Process alone; they need the support of their Champion to map out each step and go into bat for the Seller if any unexpected issues arise or your deal needs prioritizing with other stakeholders.

As uncomfortable as it may become to press your Champion for confirmation and updates for each stage, it is required. Your Champion is likely to ease your pressures by telling you they have it all under control, but easing up on thoroughly working through each stage is the opposite of what you should do.

For each stakeholder in the Paper Process, you want to ensure your Champion has confirmed that they are aware, briefed, and available for the timeframes that have been committed to.

Killer-Questions To your Champion:

"Have you worked through these stages with a solution of similar complexity/cost to mine before?"

"What things should we look out for?"

"What have you seen go wrong?"

"What things should we be doing to be on the front foot?"

The 3 Key Elements of any Paper Process

There are always three key elements of any Paper Process. They are as follows:

1. The Process
2. The People
3. The Timing

1. The Process

The Seller needs to understand the entire process to go from being the vendor of choice through to having their contractual agreements signed. Each organization will be different and have different layers of approval and authority that need satisfying.

It is essential to consider what dependencies each part of the process has. You have to ensure they are mapped out within the Go-Live Plan and are confirmed with all of the relevant stakeholders.

Once we have agreed on and approved the paperwork, we need to understand who needs to sign it, and what steps in the process need to be taken to get that person to sign.

What happens if the signer is incapacitated? I.e., they are ill. Is there someone else that can sign in their absence?

2. The People

Equally as important as the process are the people. For each step of the process, who are the people who are required to approve each stage?

Have you built reasonable contingency plans in case anyone should be delayed or unavailable at any time?

Every Seller knows a horror story of where they had meticulously built out their Paper Process only for a stakeholder to disappear on vacation, thus damaging the planned process.

3. The Timing

The last element of the Paper Process is timing. There needs to be some form of time deadline around the Paper Process. It is ideally driven by a deadline on the customer's side, but failing that, the Seller should always have a deadline they are working towards whether it is tied to resources that are being reserved for the implementation of the deal or related to a time-limited commercial offer by the Seller.

Having a deadline drives urgency on both sides and maintains momentum on the deal.

The vast majority of timelines are driven by the Seller and the timing constraints of how the organizations they represent report their financial earnings, such as a quarter or year-end. You only have to look at the close dates of any enterprise solution provider and you will notice a cluster of deals closing at the end of the quarter or year.

What has always fascinated me is how deals that slip from closing at the end of a quarter rarely tend to close within the first week of the next quarter. However, I bet that if you were able to extend the previous quarter a week the Seller would get it closed. This just proves to be more pivotal the Seller is in dictating the timing and urgency of the close.

Paper Process when in Closing Mode

The Paper Process comes into its own when sales organizations find themselves in the closing mode, such as at the end of a quarter or financial year. In these scenarios where all focus zooms into the deals left to close in the current quarter, Sellers and sales leaders can lean almost entirely on the Paper Process.

The benefit for Sellers and Sales Leaders alike is that it focuses the attention of all of the stages that need passing to get a deal closed and highlights all of the aspects that could impact the likelihood of the deal being forecasted when forecasted.

Stay on your toes

Even when you have the Paper Process entirely mapped out and confirmed by your Champion, there is always a high Risk of unanticipated factors throwing a spanner in the works. For this reason, it is crucial that you regularly seek consensus from your Champion and other stakeholders that you are engaged with that the Paper Process is still on track and you are considering all of the elements.

Paper Process and Go-Live Plan

The Go-Live Plan plays a critical part in helping to document the Paper Process.

Sellers should work with their Champion to map out each stage of the Paper Process, the dependencies of each stage, and timeframes/deadlines for completion.

As with when you initially constructed the Go-Live Plan with your Champion, you should revisit the timeframes and deadlines to ensure the Champion has full visibility of the steps ahead of you both. You have their consensus around the timelines.

Paper Process and your Sales Process

The Paper Process is a part of the sales process that cannot be passed over. It is the part of MEDDICC that can have the most significant impact on the forecast accuracy from a timings perspective.

Early-Stages:

The Paper Process is often skipped in the early stages of deals, but it shouldn't be ignored entirely as the Paper Process can have an impact on paperwork such as an NDA (Non-Disclosure Agreement).

I have seen NDA's that slow deals down as organizations cannot reach agreement on the terms.

On rare occasions, NDA's can also contain legally binding terms in areas such as intellectual property or liabilities. These types of terms are often controversial and are likely to need intervention from the legal team. I have seen NDA's grind deals to a halt at the early stages and, in some cases, kill the deal altogether.

With all of this in mind, Sellers must get on the front foot with NDA's and any other paperwork that will need to be agreed upon before a full sales engagement takes place.

As part of your discovery process, you are likely to uncover details relating to the Paper Process such as who some stakeholders will be, how their procurement and legal processes work as well as any matters that should be considered at this stage such as unusual terms or expectations.

Mid-Stages:

In the mid-stages of your sales cycle, you want to gain visibility of the Paper Process, what stages it contains, and which stakeholders will be involved.

If there are any significant stakeholders you haven't had a chance to engage with, you need to work with your Champion to plan that engagement.

Before entering into any commercial discussions, you will want to have a strong understanding of the Paper Process as some elements may need negotiating from your side and if you have already entered into commercial discussions you may have lost some of the leverage required to obtain the most favorable deal for your organization.

Mid-Stage Consensus:

The Seller needs to obtain consensus from their Champion of what the Paper Process is and that it hasn't changed from how it was detailed earlier in the sales process.

Late-Stages:

In the late stages of the deal cycle, the Seller should be immersed within the Paper Process with a clear understanding of the stages of the process, the stakeholders responsible for them, their dependencies, and the timing around each stage.

The Seller should be tracking progress against each stage in real-time within the Go-Live Plan, which should be shared with all stakeholders and regularly discussed and updated.

The Paper Process is not completed until the deal has been signed and booked against the opportunity in the Sellers CRM system.

Late-Stage Consensus:

The consensus at the late stage should all be around the confidence of your Go-Live Plan. The Seller's confidence in forecasting measures the level of confidence, their deal should be committed, and the Seller should be prepared to stand firmly on the date.

Summary Snapshot of the Paper Process in the sales process:

- Early: Can I get a brief snapshot of the Paper Process?
- Mid: Were my initial assumptions and information correct? Is there anything I need to be prepared for or anyone I need to be introduced to?

- Late: Do I fully understand the Process, People, and Timing and feel confident it is as my Go-Live Plan shows?

Summary of Paper Process

The sooner Sellers engage in the Paper Process, the sooner they can progress on the stages within it. Often different stages of the Paper Process are not dependent on each other or the progress of the deal, so items such as security approvals can be completed in the mid-stages of the deal, saving time and resources for other things dependent on the late stages.

A thoroughly executed Paper Process leads to fewer surprises and vastly improved forecast accuracy.

A word from Jack on Paper Process

Paper is evidence of commitment - As the sales process progresses, the execution of paper documents increases the commitment. It starts with a mutual NDA and progresses from there.

Elite Sellers introduce documents early - Asking to engage in the Paper Process stages early allows Sellers to test their Champion's commitment to progressing the deal.

The sooner you can work through the Paper Process, the sooner you will move your deal towards closing.

Get on the front foot and stay there - By being on the front foot with the Paper Process, you can help yourself stay there. For instance, if you get an NDA agreed upon as early as possible, it will give you a good indication of how your customer's legal department works, which will help you plan for future engagements and build trust.

IMPLICATE THE PAIN

Implicating the Pain means you have both Identified, Indicated, and Implicated the Pain your solution solves upon your customer.

P ain is a problem the customer has with their business that is serious enough that there is a need for a solution.

The severity of the pain will decipher whether the customer chooses to try and solve it. This means it's the Sellers' role to Implicate the Pain upon the customer. The level in which you can do so will define just how painful the customer finds the issue and subsequently, the amount of value your solution provides. The higher the pain, the higher the value, the higher the priority.

With so many innovative technology solutions available today, Sellers often have solutions to problems that customers didn't know they had or that could be solved. This puts extra importance on the Implication of Pain as, unlike a perceived pain, you will be responsible for uncovering, articulating, and quantifying the pain.

The 3 Types of Pain

There are many types of pain, but they generally roll up into three categories of pain.

Financial Pain: This relates to where the organization is either missing out on revenue or has higher costs relating to the pain.

The quantification of Financial Pain is likely to be dollars. Either dollars missed out on being earned or less profitable dollars being earned.

Efficiency Pain: This relates to a Pain that is occurring because something prohibits the organization from being efficient or effective.

The quantification of Efficiency Pain is usually time: the time it takes or the number of resources required for a process to occur.

People Pain: This relates to pain that impacts the People in the organization either by productivity, morale, skill, or ability.

The quantification of People Pain is often measured in the output of individuals or departments and therefore is more specific to where the pain lies. People's pain in a sales team is likely to be around ability levels that could be surfaced by poor sales results.

Another example of where People Pain could surface is in high staff turnover rates.

Who Owns the Pain?

Every pain has an owner who is ultimately responsible for it, and you need to trace the pain to the owner to ensure you uncover all parts of it and the stakeholders who are affected.

Elite Sellers build influence maps of the stakeholders within the organization they are selling to. Mapping the types of pain to stakeholders keeps you focused on what kinds of conversation you need to have and with whom.

Talk in your Customer's Language when Talking about Pain

When you uncover pain from your customer, note how they describe the pain and be sure to use the same language. This will help to resonate with the pain with other people in the organization.

If you are leading your customer in articulating the pain, then stick to industry terminology and steer clear from buzzwords as they have a habit of being seen as less credible.

Identify, Indicate, or Implicate the Pain?

The I in MEDDICC has a few definitions. A common misconception is that the 'I' is just a way of getting to the 'P' for pain. However, if you go more in-depth on it, you'll uncover that it represents the opportunity to create the most value in the entire MEDDICC methodology:

The Three I's Transition:

- i1. Identify
- i2. Indicate
- i3. Implicate

Each I represents a stage in your process to Implicate the Pain, which starts with **Identifying the Pain.** This is the stage occupied by most Sellers upon completion of some discovery with the client. Average Sellers will use this information in the selling to direct their strengths towards the pain they have identified.

Leading sales methodologies such as SPIN Selling by Neil Rackham, or Command of the Message by Force Management would refer to the where you have Identified the Pain as being the 'Situation' or the 'Before State' as with those principles you have much more work to do to surface the pain entirely.

Tactics to Identify the Pain

- Identify pain by talking about problems you have solved for other customers and expand upon them by asking if they are having the same issues.

- Suppose you can put yourself into the position of your customer's customers and can identify pain, such as a poor user experience. In that case, you can use this information to surface the pain to your customer through their customers' eyes.

The next stage in the transition is to **Indicate the Pain.** Most Sellers Indicate the Pain to their customers, by quantifying it into a document that illustrates their return on investment. Often this is presented as part of a proposal or business case.

Indicating the pain relates to the 'Problem' in SPIN Selling and the 'Negative Consequences' in Command of the Message.

By this indication of the pain, the customer is likely to know their pain and how much it costs them.

Tactics to Indicate the Pain

Work with your Champion to quantify the cost of the pain to the business and build it into a business case that shows the proposed return on investment that the customer will benefit from by implementing your solution and subsequently solving their pain.

To maximize your solution's perceived value, you need to move to the final stage of The Three I's Transition, which is to **Implicate this Pain** upon your customers, making them feel the negative impact the pain is having on their business. When done correctly, this will elevate the pain from something they may have wanted to solve in the future to something they have to address immediately.

Tactics to Implicate the Pain

- Show a glimpse into the future Utopian state that your solution can provide.

- Use two-sided discovery to make the customer live in the moment of their pain

Note: As MEDDICC is a qualification methodology, the purpose of The Three I's Transition is to help you qualify whether you have Identified, Indicated, and Implicated the Pain. Just like the rest of MEDDICC, you should apply it over the top of a sales methodology.

Uncover Pain via Discovery

It is all too easy to say the way to uncover pain is through thorough discovery. This is, of course, a true statement. As detailed in the discovery chapter, running a thorough discovery process takes more than just having a bank of good questions to ask, you need to earn the right to ask them, and that right is only given if you have built credibility.

Building credibility concerning pain comes from referencing other similar organizations that have had the same pain and how you have solved it for them. Approaching pain this way will give you credibility for being seen to have addressed the pain before, but it will also be a more open way of discussing pain with the customer instead of just firing questions at them.

Pain Creates Urgency

I've often said that the main difference between Order Takers and Elite Sellers is that Elite Sellers make deals happen in their timeframes, and Order Takers take the order when the customer places it.

Of course, Elite Sellers aren't dictating the time frame or anything that bold, but what they are doing is selling in such a manner that it creates urgency and subsequently accelerates the timeframes.

Accelerated timeframes combined with Sellers who use a qualification methodology like MEDDICC means deals that not only close quicker but are forecasted accurately as well.

Implicate the Pain in your Sales Process

If you don't uncover pain early in your sales cycle, getting to the Mid and Late-Stages is low. If you find yourself in the Mid or Late Stages and haven't uncovered pain, there is a good chance that you are wasting your time, and your deal will be lost, either to inertia or to a competitor more successful in uncovering pain. Your best-case scenario is that you can do significant discounts to get the deal done. Either way, it's not a good scenario to be in.

With this in mind, it is essential to find and track pain through all of the stages.

Early-Stages:

In the early stages, you are trying to uncover pain. The saying from the fitness world of 'No Pain No Gain' is just as true for sales.

Once you Identify pain, you want to qualify how real it is and genuinely something that you can solve. The best way to prove your hypothesis here is to see if you can find a correlation between the pain you have resolved for another organization and the pain you have uncovered.

Once you have qualified that you have Identified pain, it is time to dig deep in discovery to Indicate just how big the pain is, subsequently what is the cost to the organization and who does it impact?

Ensuring the Pain is Implicated in the early stages may mean the deal takes longer to progress to the mid-stages. Still, it is a course of action well worth taking as by Implicating the Pain as early as possible, will streamline the deal through the later stages.

You should be looking to connect how the pain is solved to the Decision Criteria and be working on adding how you uniquely solve the pain as new Decision Criteria.

Early Consensus:

In the early stages, you need to identify if there is a real pain that is not only felt by the business but that you can solve.

The Coach or Champion should confirm the existence of the pain and be able to relate to its cost to the business.

Mid-Stages:

As you move into the mid-stages of a deal, your Champion should fully understand the pain, how it impacts their business, and how your solution will help solve the pain.

The Economic Buyer should at least be aware of the pain and the cost upon the business of not solving it. Your aim should be to Implicate the Pain upon the business enough for the Economic Buyer to prioritize addressing the pain.

Mid Consensus:

There should be a consensus that the pain aligns with the Decision Criteria, and all of the stakeholders in the Decision Process are aware of how your solution uniquely solves the pain.

Late-Stages:

By the late stages of your deal, all stakeholders should be fully aware of the pain, it's costs to their business, and how your solution uniquely solves it.

Late Consensus:

Consensus on the Pain at this stage means that the customer knows that by investing in your solution, it will solve the pain, costing their business an amount that has been quantified.

They also understand how your solution is differentiated between your Competitors and the difference in results they could expect by picking an alternative solution.

Often when Sellers get into the late stages of their deal, they zoom their focus into the technical validation and working through the Paper Process, and subsequently, the pain they have implicated starts to fade. For this reason, you need to keep re-implicating the pain throughout the sales cycle.

Implicating the pain after you've won the deal

Just as with the Metrics, once you have closed the deal, you will want to remain close to the customer to be able to see the pain get solved.

Staying close will help you gather reference points for future sales and locks in your credibility with your customer, which will be useful for any future renewals, upsells, or referrals from the customer in the future.

Summary of Implicating the Pain

Ask yourself as a Seller or if you are a sales leader, ask your reps:

"Where are your current deals sat? i1? i2? or i3?"

To put it another way:

Which of the following three scenarios best describes the pain associated with your deals:

- i1 — You have identified some pain
- i2 — You have Indicated the cost of the pain to your customer
- i3 — You have implicated the pain onto your customer, and they feel the negative impact it is having upon their business

For many, these will be nuances or subtle differences, but, for those in the know, it is the difference between average, good, and Elite Sellers.

A word from Jack on Implicating the Pain

No business pain, no business - If the initial cost of doing nothing is too low, qualify out.

Find the person in power who cares about the Pain - Implicating Pain that no one in power cares about is a waste of your time. It is the fastest way to get to a "No Decision" scenario, wasting precious resources as you go.

Transfer Ownership of the Pain - By moving from Indicating the Pain to Implicating the Pain, you transfer ownership of the Pain from your hands to the customers. This is the single most significant activity you can undertake to inspire your customer to take action in your deal.

CHAMPION

The Champion is a person who is
assisting us and has power, influence,
and credibility within the customer's
organization.

Y ou may have heard the phrase "No Champion, No Deal" which is a very astute view. From my perspective, this is true. The only time I've seen deals won without a Champion is when the Seller is taking an order.

Champion or Champions?

Always Champions! The purpose of working with a Champion is that when we align ourselves with them, they help us make progress with our deal and give visibility into previously dark areas.

The more Champions you have, the more you will be able to align yourself with your buyers while uncovering more useful information.

That said, generally, most deals tend to have one primary Champion. Who the primary Champion is may shift through the deal as you uncover new stakeholders and values and priorities change. Elite Sellers can manage and maintain their relationships with all influential stakeholders.

For the purpose of ease of articulation, this chapter will relate to a singular Champion.

Coach or Champion?

Similar to Implicating the Pain The first C in MEDDICC has a transition; from Coach > Champion.

The definition of a Coach is someone who is friendly and gives useful information about your deal. Most Champions should start as Coach's and evolve into Champions once you have qualified them. However, not all Coaches can become Champions.

The Criteria of a Champion:

To Evolve a Coach to a Champion, they require the following explicit criteria:

1. A Champion has power and influence
2. A Champion acts as an internal Seller for you
3. A Champions has a vested interest in your success

> *"A Champion without Power and Influence*
> *is just a Coach."*

Let's go a little deeper on each part of the criteria:

1. A Champion has power and influence

The most critical criteria that a Champion must have is Power and Influence. Without this, you have someone unable to be more than a Coach, unlike criteria 2 & 3 on this list in which can be evolved from Coach to Champion.

Power and Influence doesn't necessarily mean seniority

A common misconception is that a Champion needs to have a certain level of seniority to be a Champion. While rank and a person's Power and Influence are often linked, they aren't exclusively so. In today's rapidly evolving world, the most experienced and tenured professionals rely on the input of junior executives more than ever before, and often what these junior executives lack in career tenure and seniority related influence they make up for by having domain expertise.

2. A Champion acts as an internal Seller for you

A Champion sells for you. There are three types of internal sell that your Champion should do for you:

The Public

The Private

The Competitor

The Public Champion Sell

There are likely to be many meetings in which you and your Champion are in with other stakeholders. Within these meetings, your Champion can sell publicly on your behalf.

Your Champions selling can be both Subtle and Bold, for example:

A **Subtle Sell** could be the Champion expanding on a point to personalize it to the specific circumstance of the organization. An example of this could be:

Seller: "We work with Acme INC, who uses our Talent Module to manage unwanted attrition. We have helped them reduce unwanted attrition by 30%."

Champion: "Jen in HR told me that attrition is a focus for them this year."

A **Bold Sell** is not subtle at all, the Champion is proactively backing your value and is sticking her neck out to ensure the point hits. An example:

Seller: "This technology would eradicate the need for you to rely on third-party affiliates to drive traffic."

Champion: "That would save us $10million a year alone…!"

The Private Champion Sell

The most critical selling your Champion can do for you is when you are not there.

When your value gets challenged in private, your Champion must step up to defend you. Their defense has to be credible. The best way to enable your Champion to be credible in selling for you is to arm them with the I and the M from MEDDICC - Pain, and Metrics.

The Competitor Champion Sell

As will be defined in the Competition chapter, there are many kinds of Competitors for your solution. The most common will be another vendor who is offering a similar solution. This Competitor is likely to do three things to attack your solution:

1. They will talk about the unique value that only they can offer

2. They will attack you or your solution outright with FUD

3. They will lay traps for your solution to fall into

Whether these attacks are bold or subtle, your Champion will need to defend these attacks while also counter-attacking by laying traps for you and highlighting the unique value that only you have.

Note: It isn't advised that you coach your Champion to be outwardly negative about your competition. It is always much better to get your Champion to focus on your strengths and the unique parts of your solution related to the Pains you have Implicated and the Metrics that support them.

3. A Champions have a vested interest in your success

If we fail, they fail.

If we win, they win.

Put simply, a Champions success should have some form of alignment with your success.

Their desire for success with you could be external such as wanting to work with your solution to elevate their career prospects or internal where it will enhance their chances of promotion or to receive a bonus. It is essential you uncover what is in it for them, and keep that front of mind when engaging with your Champion.

Elite Sellers manage to stay aligned to their Champion's success without making their Champion feel uncomfortable or bias for supporting them.

There will likely come a time in your deal where you will rely on your Champion to stick their neck out or go the extra mile for you. Having strong alignment with their win will help encourage this when you need it.

Build Your Champion

Once you have evolved your Coach into a Champion, your work has only just begun. Elite Sellers know that having a Champion isn't binary and that they need to continually work on building their Champions to enable their full potential.

Your focus for how you build your Champion falls into two parts:

1. Solution

2. Political

The fundamental difference between these two parts is education. Building your Champion on your solution requires you to work closely with your Champion with you educating them on your solution and the value it provides. Whereas, building your Champion on the Political side requires them to educate you about the Political landscape of their business.

Both parts are equally important but require very different tactics. Let's take a closer look at the required tactics you need below:

1. Solution

Build Credibility with your Champion by Value Selling

The best way to build credibility is by being consistent, reliable, and by demonstrating genuine value.

An excellent strategy to demonstrate value is through a thorough two-sided discovery process.

Using two-sided discovery will help to Implicate the Pain on the customer—then underpinning the Pain with Metrics that specifically refer to where you provide value and how the value is derived, with examples of where you have done it before.

Educate your Champion on MEDDICC

Using MEDDICC to coach your Champion is a great place to start.

The best parts of MEDDICC for coaching your Champion are Metrics, Decision Criteria, and Implicate the Pain. These three parts of MEDDICC give you the basis to educate your Champion on the elements of your solution's value with the pain being quantified by the Metrics, which needs to be related to your solutions unique differentiators that offer the value.

Once you have this clearly articulated with your Champion, you need to work with them on these elements becoming requirements within the Decision Criteria.

Make your Champion Pitch Perfect

Your Champion is likely to have to pitch your solution internally when you aren't there. It is one hundred percent your job to coach your Champion to ensure their pitch is perfect, and if it isn't, it is your job to work on them to improve it.

A few tips for doing this are as follows:

KISS - No, It's not what you are thinking! KISS is an acronym for Keep it Simple Silly. It means that you need to keep the pitch simple so the Champion can grasp it with ease. Unlike you, their day job isn't to sell your solution, nor do they have the years of experience and training that you do, so we need to keep it simple. MEDDICC is your friend here. Get your Champion to stick to the elements of MEDDICC relating to the solution, and you will keep them on track and consistent with your message.

Using MEDDICC in this way will also have two super by-products:

1. You will be qualifying the MEDDICC of the deal with your Champion. If you have got something wrong, they will speak out.

2. You'll be inadvertently helping your Champion absorb the value of your solution in a quantified manner that aligns with their Decision Criteria.

The Three Why's - Another way to keep the Champions articulation of your solution on track is to use the Three Why's:

3. Why should they buy *your solution, e.g., Human Resources Management Software?*

4. Why should they buy from *Your Company?*

5. Why should they buy it now?

Having a Champion able to answer these three questions, articulately will make them a very effective internal Seller.

Build their Documentation - Have you ever seen when a customer builds their documentation about your solution? It is rarely good, and as much as it is useful as a test to see how they are articulating your solution, it is much better to give them the documentation they need to build the solution.

Most Sellers will always send the deck after a meeting, but Elite Sellers know that adapting the deck to the preferred format of their Champion will help their Champion maximize the accuracy of their pitch. This process will involve removing the branding and styling your content, so it doesn't feature any of your solutions branding.

It is also beneficial to give your Champion value-based documentation, such as any documents that calculate the return on investment or business case you have built.

*Note: I have heard Sellers display resistance to sending editable documentation, preferring to send rigid PDFs instead for fear of their Champion sharing it with their competition. **PSST! If they do this, then they aren't your Champion!** If it is a real fear, then you can explain to your Champion ahead of sending it how vital confidentiality is. This is an excellent method to build mutual trust with your Champion.*

Reconnect your Champion to their Needs - Often, your customer may lose touch with the main reason why they are engaging with you throughout the stages of the buying process. Reconnecting your Champion to their needs will help your deal stay a priority.

If All Else Fails Lean on your References - If you are struggling to make progress with your Champion, then falling back to your references is a reliable backup tactic. To do this link, the pain you have implicated to another customer who had a similar pain for which you solved. Use your reference customers Metrics to illustrate and quantify the value you delivered to your reference customer.

Note: while enthusiastic Champions are great, they mustn't be too enthusiastic towards your solution internally as it may cause them to lose credibility internally as they may seem biased. The best way for solving this is actually to focus on keeping coaching your Champion. The more armed they are with reliable information, the more genuine their pitch will appear.

2. Politics

Build Credibility with your Champion via Networking

Another way to build credibility is by Networking. Introducing your Champion to other people in your network is an excellent way of creating some social proofing around yourself.

There are three different kinds of people to consider:

Other Champions with the organization: while it is unlikely if you are working with a small organization that you will be able to introduce them to someone they don't know or who isn't aware of your deal, in bigger organizations it is a common occurrence for there to be multiple stakeholders and potential Champions who aren't aware of each other.

Champions from other Similar Organizations: Introducing your Champion to their peers in other similar organizations is a great way to introduce references for your solution while also helping your Champion to increase their network. Another type of external Champion could be an industry expert or partner who can add further value to your engagement.

Introduce your Executive Team: At the right time introducing senior executives from your company to your Champion goes a long way to demonstrate your commitment to their success.

Build Trust

Trust is a critical element in building a Champion. A Champion who trusts the Seller will always work harder for you. They'll go into bat harder for you and be happier to give you information, good, bad, or ugly.

Building Trust with a Champion takes time and comes from being consistent, reliable, and honest.

A key component of trust and the Achilles heel of many Sellers is honesty. Obviously, being honest with your customers is the ethical and right thing to do. Still, far too often, Sellers shy away from outright honesty for fear that, by doing so, uncovers a shortfall that reflects poorly upon them.

The truth is that most of the time if you are honest about a negative matter, your honesty will win you far more credibility than you will have lost by raising the negative.

Friendly, not necessarily Friends

You don't need to be friends with your Champion, but you do need to be friendly with them.

Making friends with the Champion is a strategy high on the Order Takers to-do list. It works for Order Takers as their strategy is to be reactive and be seen as a trusty partner. However, Elite Sellers know that they need to be pro-active. Sometimes, that means putting themselves in an awkward position with their Champion, where friendship has to come secondary to getting the deal done.

An example of this would be if you ask your Champion to introduce you to the Economic Buyer, and they decline, they politely request that you leave it to them to deal with the Economic Buyer. Order Takers not wanting to disagree and cause an upset will agree to these terms, whereas an elite Seller knows that without access to the Economic Buyer, her chances of getting the deal done are diminished.

The best Seller and Champion partnerships I see are out-come-driven and orientate around the mutual gain both parties will obtain from the success of the deal going ahead.

Tools to Build Champions

There are many tools that Elite Seller will use to build their Champions. The skill comes not only in knowing when to use the tools but in the how.

Champion Building Event - These events can take many shapes, from smaller, more intimate events such as a tasting experience at a restaurant through to a VIP experience at an industry event like an awards show. There are a few elements that a good Champion Building Event needs:

- It has to be a relatively exclusive event to give your Champion that VIP feeling.

- If you have invited multiple organizations to attend, ensure you have a good split of existing customers and prospective customers. My advice would be to split them 50/50. If places are limited, it is better to give up your seat to a happy existing customer. They will be much more credible at selling your solution in this environment than you will be.

- No business chat! The purpose of the event isn't to ambush your Champion with sales pitches. It is to give them a taster into the experience of being a customer of yours.

Champion Email/Letter - A tool that can often be useful is to write to someone senior to your Champion to state what a professional job they are doing. This can win favor with your Champion but should be used with caution; it may seem like you are going above the head of your Champion (which may be the point of the letter). Be sure to be conscious of how the message is likely to be perceived by all parties.

Elevate their Career - Elevating your Champion's career is a fantastic tool to make your Champion benefit from your audience. Subsequently, they'll associate working with your company with their success.

Examples of this are:

- Invite your Champion to speak at an event you are hosting
- Invite your Champion onto a Podcast
- Interview your Champion for an industry magazine, or blog post

Note: Using your company profile to raise your Champions profile is likely to alert your competition. You need to prepare for the possible outcome of your competition reaching out. This is why you need to lay effective traps for your competition, at every stage!

Counter Champion

Elite Sellers know that their Champion may not be the only Champion in the business. They are just as likely to have a Counter Champion representing their competition, whether they are a Champion for a competitive vendor or a competing project.

The best way to approach a scenario where you have a Counter Champion is to approach the situation just as is explained in the Competition chapter of this book, which focuses on

Testing Champions

I have lost count of the number of times I've heard Sellers reference their Champion only for it to become immediately evident that the Champion is neither qualified nor tested. Put simply; an untested Champion isn't a Champion.

"An untested Champion isn't a Champion."

Remember the criteria of a Champion:

1. A Champion has power and influence
2. A Champion acts as an internal Seller for you
3. A Champions has a vested interest in your success

Each of these criteria needs to be tested.

1. Testing your Champions Power and Influence:

As mentioned earlier in this chapter, a Champion's influence isn't necessarily defined by their seniority, which means you will have to work much harder than just glimpsing at the customer's org chart to figure out who has power.

Questions to Ask:

Look closely at their responsibilities:

- What are they measured on?
- Who are they accountable to?
- Who was involved in creating the Decision Criteria?
- Who is included in the Decision Process?
- What resources are they in control of or have access to?

Killer-Question: Ask your Champion about the last time they worked on a deal like yours. Ask them about the steps they took to get the deal done and what obstacles they had to overcome. Their answers to these questions will help you quickly identify the level of power and influence they are operating have.

Check your network Do you have mutual connections to your Champion?

Has anyone in your network worked with them before? Or have they been involved in selling to them?

Sellers tend to overlook the value of other vendors' engagement. The chances are there is a lot you can learn, not just about whether your Champion has Power and Influence, but about dealing with the organization you are selling to.

One critical element of Power and Influence that a Champion needs is regarding the Economic Buyer. They need to have access and the power and influence to be able to get you access.

2. Testing your Champion is selling internally for you

The quickest and most efficient way of testing your Champion on whether they have been selling internally for you is to ask them the following question:

> *"In the conversations you've been having about my solution internally, has anyone raised any concerns or negative opinions?"*

This is two birds with one stone question. Not only will you be able to identify if your Champion has stuck up for you and 'sold internally,' but you are also going to be able to identify potential detractors or even your Competitions Champion.

If a Champion is selling internally, they are likely to come to you with questions and requests to help them. They may want to introduce you to someone new, or for you to send them documentation.

By contrast, if you notice that your Champion isn't leaning on you for any help, the chances are they aren't doing much selling for you internally.

A crucial part of your relationship with your Champion is their role in selling internally for you. A Champion will be open to you coaching them to be better able to articulate your value. Your Champion should be open to your help. If they are not, then they have failed the test of a Champion.

3. Testing your Champion has a Vested Interest in your success

We know that our Champion has to have a vested interest in our success, but getting to what drives that interest is key. My advice is to ask your Champion outright:

"What happens if we don't win?"

Based on their answer will help you define your next question, but you may need to be more specific and pointed with your follow up. The conversation could look like this:

You: "What happens if we don't win?"

Champion: "It'll be a shame, but I guess we'll try to carry on as we did before."

You: "What will that mean for you?"

Champion: "Well, my team will be stretched, and we may have a tougher time hitting our annual numbers."

You: "will that impact your bonus?"

Champion: "Yes."

BINGO. We now know financial gain is their vested interest. You could swap your last question for

"Would that impact your chances of being promoted?"

OR

"Would that impact your chances of you winning awards?"

This will come down to your intuition and understanding of your Champion to uncover just what their vested interest is, but it'll be there.

Your Champion should be working with you towards your success. They should trust your guidance in methods to help with that success. An excellent example of where a Champion can help a Seller is by introducing them to the Economic Buyer. A good Champion knows that the Seller is the best person to pitch the Economic Buyer, and having them engaged will be positive for their deal.

A Champion should share confidential information, good, bad, and ugly. Useful areas of information they can share is how you are scoring against the Decision Criteria, and critically how you compare to your competitors.

Another way your Champion will show you that they have a vested interest in your success is how they behave when things aren't going your way. Do they lean in and help? Or do they passively stand by? A Champion won't want you to lose without a fight.

In summary, a tested Champion should be pro-actively helping you win. They should help you refine your MEDDICC, and they should help you access essential stakeholders like the Economic Buyer, they should move obstacles out of your way and be open to your coaching and ideas to move the deal on.

Champion Red Flags

There are different types of Red Flags you can get from your Champion. Some Red Flags point to areas that need work on developing your Champion, some point to areas that you need to observe, and some need tackling asap.

No Buying Experience If your Champion has never purchased a solution similar to yours in complexity or cost, then this is a Red Flag. Regardless of how closely they fit the three qualifying criteria of a Champion, this is a Red Flag that you should consider at every stage with your deal.

Not run any similar deals in their current company If your Champion has never bought a similarly priced solution at their current company, this is a Red Flag. It means you will need to work with your Champion to seek out what the Decision and Paper Process is pro-actively. Ideally, they can introduce you to someone who has been through the Decision and Paper Process with the company to discover the details of the processes.

They won't leave their lane Real Champions get it done! If an obstacle in their way, they work hard to overcome it even if stepping into someone else's lane.

They Don't Tell you Anything you Don't Already Know One of the best tests of a Champion is how much they coach you. Champions tell you everything, good bad and ugly. Suppose you review your communication with your Champion and realize they haven't told you anything you didn't already know. In that case, there is an issue, either they aren't sharing all of the information with you or aren't that well connected to the Decision Process.

Champion and Go-Live Plan

Your Go-Live Plan has two owners - you and your Champion, and it is your Champion who dictates how successful your Go-Live Plan will be.

Your Go-Live Plan should be introduced to your Champion at the earliest opportunity. Not necessarily to start filling it out, but to set the ground rules of how you work and your expectations from your Champion. It is a great way to qualify how strong your Champion is likely to be.

I have seen Elite Sellers bring out their Go-Live Plan at the end of a successful first meeting to get their Champions buy-in and set expectations around time frames and get a view of the Decision and Paper Process early on from the customer.

As your deal progresses, you can use your Go-Live Plan as a map with your Champion to stakeholders that they will need to introduce you to as well as milestones you need to work through together.

Champion and Procurement

Your Champion can help you by setting up your engagement with Procurement to be based on the business case you have built. This will keep the conversation orientated around value rather than just cost.

Anecdote: Once I was in a deal with a major retailer and my Champion told me that the Procurement team gets measured on the percentage in which they can reduce the cost put in front of them. The Champion explained that procurement's target was to achieve a reduction of 15% or more. My Champion advised me that my pricing should allow for an additional 15% margin to enable us to have a swift and productive engagement with Procurement.

Without this intel from my Champion, My deal would have stalled with Procurement, or I'd have lost a 15% margin.

Likewise, if you had no pricing guidance from your Champion and added 15% to your price to build a buffer for procurement, it could make your cost too high even to get taken in front of procurement.

A good Champion will know which are the usual sticking points and easy wins for you with Procurement and can help prime you for success once you are engaged.

Remember: Procurement are professionals. While many Sellers have experience in dealing with Procurement and may have benefitted from various training courses, the fact remains that Procurement deals with Sellers all day every day. You are unlikely to be able to outplay them at their own game. Therefore the best strategy is also the most credible: Talk in the language of value underpinned by a rock-solid business case.

Champion and Legal

Like Procurement, your Champion is critical in helping you progress your contract with the customer's legal department.

Depending on how complex your solution and legal terms are will depend on how lengthy the legal process will be. There are likely to be multiple disputed points, often known as redlines. Your Champion can help you decipher between which redlines are real show stoppers and which can be negotiated.

Champion and your Sales Process

Your Champion will be with you at every step of your sales process, playing a critical part in guiding you through the stages.

Early-Stages:

In the early stages of your sales process, your focus will be on discovery, and one of your first tasks should be to try and identify potential Champions.

Identify your Champion - It is unlikely that anyone you identify will be a Champion from the start of your engagement. They will most likely be indifferent. It is your job to start building these people into Champions by uncovering their pains and translating them into the value that your solution will provide, always underpinned by references.

Qualify with your Champion - As soon as you have identified a potential Champion, you need to start working with them on your deal's qualification process. Elite Sellers know that their success depends on prioritizing their time and that not all deals are winnable. Qualifying that they are in the right deals is a critical part of their success.

In the qualification stages, you should be working with your Champion to uncover the pain and the Decision Criteria.

Qualify your Champion - Once you know the deal is worth exploring further, you need to qualify your Champion. You should be looking to qualify against the three criteria of a Champion.

MEDDICC and your Champion - Use MEDDICC to focus on qualifying your deal with your Champion. In particular, dig into the pain and Metrics and then identify what the Decision Criteria and Process looks like, as well as who the stakeholders are, including the Economic Buyer.

At a high level, you should be looking to uncover the following information within the early stages:

- *Metrics* - Your Champion should help you confirm the Metrics you have identified are applicable.

- *Economic Buyer* - Your Champion should help you identify who the Economic Buyer is, and you should discuss an introduction.

- *Decision Criteria* - Your Champion should be able to explain the Decision Criteria to you if they have one, or work closely with you to define one if they don't.

- *Decision Process* - Your Champion should take you through the Decision Process if they have one or help you understand how the Decision Process flows.

- *Implicate Pain* - Your Champion should be open to you, discovering where their pain is and helping you quantify it.

- *Competition* - Your Champion should be able to give you some information about who your competition is

Test your Champion - In the early stages of your deal, you need to test your Champion to establish whether they are a fully qualified Champion. If they are not, you need to prioritize building them into a Champion or finding a new Champion.

Early Consensus:

The qualification and testing stages should help you gain an early consensus about the status of your Champion.

Be upfront with your Champion as to the importance of their role in your deal. A proven strategy I have seen work is to say:

> *"Champion, normally when I am working on a project like this, I need someone to act as a Champion for me; what they do is help me understand the criteria and process in which you will go through to make a decision. It helps me to ensure we focus on the right things and make everything as efficient as possible for you. I think you could be that person for me. What do you think?"*

Their answer to this question may tell you more than any of the work you have done to qualify or test them thus far. Yet, so many Sellers avoid being upfront. I talk more about this in the Epilogue.

Mid-Stages:

In the mid-stages of your deal, your Champion should be fully qualified and tested and be well underway in selling internally for you. At this stage, you should be working with your Champion on refining your value proposition, that directly aligns with the pain you have implicated, which is underpinned by the Metrics to the customer's Decision Criteria.

Your Champion should be working with you to align a Go-Live Plan in conjunction with their Decision Process while ensuring you have engagement with all of the right stakeholders, including the Economic Buyer.

Your Champion will help you kick start any internal processes that may slow the deal down at later stages. Processes such as:

Reference Process

Technical Validation Process

Security Process

Legal Process

Procurement Process

Your Champion should help you build a defense against your competition, working together with you to lay effective traps.

Mid Consensus:

By the mid-stage of your deal, there should be no doubt around the quality of your Champion. You should have identified all possible Red Flags and be working with your Champion to overcome them.

Your Champion should be pro-actively working with you on your deal by selling internally and updating you regarding all matters relating to you, good bad and ugly.

When obstacles come up, your Champion should be right beside you working through them.

Late-Stages:

By the late stages of your deal, your Champion's work on the solution side of your deal should be switching from a selling approach to an evangelist approach where they should be trying to get people excited about your solution.

The Go-Live Plan should be connecting the dots of what happens between this stage and when the customer goes live to ensure resources on both sides are ready to get going once the contract is signed.

Meanwhile, as you work through the closing stages of your deal, your Champion should be there to assist and guide you through the final steps of the Decision and Paper Process.

Late Consensus:

Late-Stage Consensus should just be a matter of running through the remaining stages of the Decision and Paper Process. You should have this illustrated within your Go-Live Plan.

Summary Snapshot of in the sales process:
- Early: Should I be in this deal? Are you my Champion?
- Mid: My Champion and I are working side by side to win this deal.
- Late: My Champion is guiding me through the close, step by step.

Champion after you've won the deal

Once an Elite Seller closes a deal, they ensure that the solution becomes the success they have promised it to be.

While you will rarely be the main point of contact between your company and your customer going forward, you should stay engaged throughout any implementation and beyond to ensure it's a success. Because you know there will be valuable data and learning points along the way.

Elite Sellers know that their Champion for the deal they have just closed can be a future Champion at other companies for them in the future, whether it is an employee or a reference.

Capture the success

Once your solution is live, the best practice is to follow-up to ensure the customer is following the Metrics that you set out.

If you have clearly defined the Metrics, they should act as an ideal reference point for how valuable your solution is. Elite Sellers will use these data points with approval from their Champion as a reference for future deals they are working on and, in an ideal situation, will capture them into a quote or case study from their Champion.

Summary of Champion

"No Champion, No Deal" - it's been a true saying for as long as the term 'Champion' has been in sales. Hopefully, this chapter goes to show you the full potential a Champion can have on your deal and gives some guidance on how to get them there.

It's not always straight forward

Building and Coaching Champions isn't always an easy process. This chapter offers lots of advice on the subject, but its implementation can be challenging if the Champion is reluctant to be coached. This is not uncommon, and the best way to keep moving forward is to stay authentic and consistent with the advice in this chapter. Once you have identified a Champion, focus on building them up. However, if you are consistently failing to find or build a Champion in your deal, qualify out.

Put simply, it is better to qualify out if you can't identify a Champion than to try and persevere without one.

Your success as a Seller will correlate closely to how effective you are at identifying, qualifying, testing, and building Champions.

A Word from Jack on Champion's

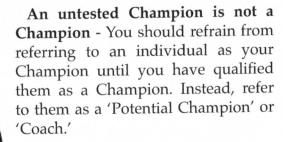

An untested Champion is not a Champion - You should refrain from referring to an individual as your Champion until you have qualified them as a Champion. Instead, refer to them as a 'Potential Champion' or 'Coach.'

This approach focuses on qualifying the Champion and doesn't allow complacency to creep in with assumptions of a Champion's worthiness.

Champions are comfortable with the uncomfortable - A Champion will work with you to overcome objections and blockers. If you find your Champion creating objections and blockers, they are most likely not a true Champion, and you need to re-evaluate.

No Champion is better than having a faux Champion - There is only one thing worse than not having a Champion, and that is having a faux Champion. This person pretends to play the Champion's role, but behind the scenes is not acting in your best interest.

Another common trait of the Faux Champion is to keep you away from the Economic Buyer.

COMPETITION

The Competition is any person,
vendor, or initiative competing for the
same funds or resources you are.

Your Competition could be any individual, initiative, or vendor competing for the same funds or resources you are.

Types of Competition

A list of possible Competition could be:

- Rival solutions - Your natural competitors
- Other projects/initiatives that require the same funds or resources
- The organization's internal team building their own solution
- Inertia - The organization opting to do nothing

Each of these types of Competition requires a different approach:

Rival Solutions:

The most common type of Competition will come from rival solutions. Whether you class them as Competition or not, if you frequently find them featuring in the same deals or they are trying to solve the same Pain as you, then they are a rival solution.

The truth is that Sellers often get way too caught up on their rivals, and it takes their eye off the prize. MEDDICC is the perfect methodology to keep you focused on what will win you the deal.

So instead of obsessing over your rival's shortfalls, instead focus on highlighting your strengths. Do this by Implicating the Pain and underpinning it with rock-solid Metrics, both of which deliver solidly against the Decision Criteria. In the meantime, coach your Champion on your unique differentiators, relating them to the Metrics and Decision Criteria.

If you focus your efforts on building a value proposition that is unique to your solution, your rival simply will not be able to compete.

Your goal should be to build such a clear proposition that when your customer asks you a challenging question about your competition, your response is simply to highlight the unique differentiators of your solution, how they are a requirement within the Decision Criteria, and the Metrics you will be using to measure their value.

Building Internally

The Build versus Buy debate has been raging for as long as technology providers have existed. While the invention of cloud computing and flexible open platforms have reduced the likelihood of an organization trying to build their own solution, it is still a genuine consideration in many sectors.

It is crucial to keep in mind that the Build versus Buy debate is often as much a political one as it is technical. For this reason, you must get to the bottom of the rationale for wanting to Build versus Buy.

A common advantage of building versus buying is that you have full control over the solution's specifications. You are not confined by the current functionality nor the future roadmap of a provider. This comes at a high cost in terms of resources, and secondly, in terms of the time it will take to build, test, and roll out the solution.

Another less common reason that organizations want to Build is that they want to maintain the solution's intellectual property. This is more common when the solution is customer-facing, and the organization feels as though it is core to their offering or brand. An example would be how most consumer apps build their apps rather than build on top of a platform.

Once you have identified the rationale for the self-build argument, you have to qualify whether it is an opportunity worth pursuing. While your qualification should begin with whether technically you provide the best solution, you will also need to qualify whether you can win the political battle. This will come down to how much power and influence your Champion has versus the instigator of the Build initiative.

Other Projects/Priorities:

There have never been so many opportunities for organizations to improve their business as there is today. As a Seller, you have more competition from other initiatives and projects than you ever had before.

Your job is to convince your customer that they are best to invest their resources in you. Once more, the Metrics can help you uncover and illustrate your solution as being the best 'bang for their buck' when it comes to weighing up which project to invest their resources in.

Inertia:

Inertia is when the customer decides to do nothing and remain unchanged.

A task I often ask my peers in sales leadership to look into is how many of their Closed Lost deals have gone on to implement a competitive solution? What I usually find is that the majority of Closed Lost deals don't implement a solution.

The above set off alarm bells when you consider how much effort you put into your selling. How much more productive could you be if you were better able to qualify a likelihood of inertia?

Great news - MEDDICC is ideal for uncovering whether your deal is heading towards inertia.

Signs your Deal is Heading for Inertia

- The customer is seemingly unwilling or unenthusiastic to build out the Metrics
- You are unable to engage with the Economic Buyer
- The Decision Criteria is undefined and/or there is no Decision Process

- You haven't been able to Identify Pain strong enough to make an impact upon the organization
- You are single-threaded and/or are failing at finding other stakeholders interested in sponsoring your deal
- There is no compelling event

If you find yourself with any of the above signals in your deal, then it is time to get real with yourself. Without a radical change, your deal is on the fast path to inertia, and you may be better qualifying out and focusing your time on a better-qualified deal.

Despite inertia being most Seller's biggest competitor, many Sellers still don't know about it, such as in one interview, the candidate asked:

"Who is your biggest competitor?"

Answer:

"Inertia."

In the second interview, the Interviewee, keen to show he had done his research, stated:

"I tried to research inertia, but I couldn't find anything about them online... How do you spell it?"

Do Not Knock the Competition

"There are two ways to have the tallest building in town. One is to tear everyone else's building down, and the other is to build your building taller."
-Jim Rohn, US Author

When I first came into sales, not knocking the Competition was described as the first rule of sales. However, today, it seems its place in the moral code of sales seems to have faded. I regularly hear from customers that our Competition has been bad-mouthing us, and from what I can tell, customers rarely receive Competition bad-mouthing well, and why would they? If the customer has invited your Competition to participate in an evaluation, then by bad-mouthing them, you question your customer's judgment.

For instance, imagine you are going to buy a new car, and you have narrowed your choice down to a BMW or a Mercedes, and in BMW, the salesperson finds out that you are also evaluating a Mercedes, so he spends the time that he could be using to tell you about how great BMW is by instead talking about how bad Mercedes is. Do you think you'll come away convinced to buy a BMW? I doubt it.

If you are confident in your solution, keep your focus on your strengths. This doesn't mean that you do not highlight weaknesses that your Competition has; it just means that you do it in such a manner that it builds your value rather than attempts to knock your Competition.

An example could be if you are selling to a global organization. You uncover that, in China, their users require Chinese languages within the interface, which you know is a unique feature that only your solution provides. Imagine, instead of going straight to highlighting that your Competition doesn't have this functionality, you zoom in on the value that having Chinese languages will provide to the local team and help quantify it into your business case. At this point, you ask whether this functionality is included within the Decision Criteria. By doing this, you will have set an effective trap for your Competition without saying a single disparaging thing about them. Better still, you have added a unique differentiator that you have also been able to quantify to the Decision Criteria.

What if the Competition Has Been Knocking You?

If you hear directly or get the sense that your Competition has been knocking you, don't panic. Do not lower yourself to their level by participating in a tit for tat counter-argument. Instead, take the high road; you can even compliment your Competition; nothing will disarm their attack and underpin how confident you are in your strengths than if you can turn around and say, "They are quite a good solution."

An example of this happened recently in a meeting with one of the fastest-growing Fintech companies in the world.

One of my Sellers had brought me into a final meeting, where we were head to head with our biggest competitor. We were told that they would be selecting a vendor following the meeting as they had already met our competitor earlier that day.

Throughout the meeting, a suspected Counter Champion kept asking questions intended to throw us off-course and highlight some concerns about us to the broader group. It was evident that this individual had been fed things to ask from our competitor. The competitor in question always used the same FUD (Fear, Uncertainty, and Doubt), oblivious to how easy it was for us to disprove it. We, of course, did swiftly while also calling out the elephant in the room, which was that our competitor had fed all of these negatives.

We said:

"We know that competition name mentions this a lot, and the reason is this..."

We explained why they say what they do and why it isn't an accurate criticism from our perspective.

It was clear that this had had a positive impact on the room, and it relieved tensions; it also put out in the open that our Competition had been trying to lay FUD against us.

Towards the end of the meeting, a partner working with the customer who was favorable to our solution spoke up and suggested:

> *"As we have some time left, and* **Competitor Name** *has clearly been stating negative things about your solution, perhaps you would like to tell us some things about them?"*

At this point, many Sellers would be thinking, "BINGO!" And begin rolling out their competitive differences deck to show just how much better their solution is. However, in this instance, we didn't do that, we instead said:

> *"Thank you, but I'll politely decline the opportunity.* **Competitor Name** *has a good solution, and when it comes to choosing them or us, some people choose us, and some people choose them. On this occasion, I happen to believe that you should pick us because of* **The Unique Value Identified***. Besides, nobody ever enjoys it when a vendor knocks their competition, let alone when it turns into a tit for tat discussion".*

Instead, we used the time to summarize why we felt our solution uniquely solved their business objectives and reiterated how it aligned with their Decision Criteria.

When the meeting wrapped up and we were heading to the elevators, a gentleman from the meeting we hadn't had much engagement with came to us and said that he liked what we said when we were asked about our Competition. He thanked us, and we left. The next day, we were made their vendor of choice, and today, they are a very important customer who has helped us win many more customers in the FinTech sector.

Competitive Strategy

Despite it not being advisable to knock the competition outwardly, you must have a Competitive Strategy to ensure you stay on the front foot when you are up against Competition.

There are three areas of your Competition to consider:

- Political: Who internally within the customer is aligned towards or is favorable to the Competition?

- Technical: How does our solution match up against the technical elements of the Decision Criteria?

- Commercial: How are we articulating our solution's unique value and/or the lost value of not selecting our solution?

Before starting to build your Competitive Strategy, you must know who and what you are up against. You should look to be able to answer these questions:

-Political:

- Who is your competition? Are they known to you?

- How were they engaged? Before you? At the same time? After? What were the circumstances of their engagement?

- Do they have a Champion? Who is their Champion? Is their Champion stronger than yours?

-Technical:

- Do you know their strengths and weaknesses?

- Do you see evidence of their presence? In the Decision Criteria, or any ad-hoc questions or traps that you are coming across?

-Commercial:

- How do you usually compare commercially?

- What areas of value do you have over your Competition? Are they in the Decision Criteria? If not, can you get them added?

Once you have some clarity on those questions, it is time to build out your Competitive Strategy. I find the best way to do this is to use a document to capture the important data points. I call this document The Competitive Strategy Plan:

The Competitive Strategy Plan

The Competitive Strategy Plan is for internal use and not intended to be shown to the customer, although if you have a particularly strong Champion, you could talk it through with them.

The plan breaks into the following sections:

Strengths - This section is for you to list your strengths over your Competition.

Weaknesses - This section is for you to list your weaknesses to your Competition.

Listing out both your strengths and weaknesses will help you to surface them to the front of your mind, which will be useful for building your strategy out on the rest of the plan.

Note: This Strengths and Weaknesses exercise should be built exclusively for the deal you are working on entirely. Only include relevant strengths and weaknesses.

Political - This section is for you to list the Political considerations concerning your Competition. Which stakeholders are likely to be favorable or open to their approach? Do they have a Champion?

Whose Champion is more influential? What is your plan to circumnavigate any strengths you see your competition has?

Technical - In this section, you should detail how you and your Competition's solutions stack up against the Decision Criteria's technical elements.

You should be looking for gaps to be added to the Strengths and Weaknesses sections of the Competitive Strategy Plan.

The Technical part of your Competitive Strategy Plan should clearly show how your solution aligns with the Decision Criteria better than the Competition.

Commercial - This section is for identifying any Commercial information relating to your Competition. You may know how their pricing model works and whether it will be favorable.

The Commercial section is also where you should highlight the value of any competitive differentiation you have identified to showcase the value they will lose if they do not select your solution.

Traps - Once you have identified your Strengths and Weaknesses, you can start to build out Traps that will highlight your Strengths and your Competition's Weaknesses.

Counter-Traps- Keep in mind that your Competition's Seller is just as likely to be setting Traps for you to fall into as you are for them.

Most Sellers are equipped to counter the Traps from their Competition, but often, by this point where they have to defend themselves, the damage has already been done.

By planning out the likely Traps your Competition are to set against you in your Competitive Strategy Plan, you can get on the front foot to defuse them before they even get laid.

For example, let's take a look at the age-old confrontation of Best-of-Breed solutions versus a Platform debate.

The Platform provider may try to lay traps where the Best-of-Breed solution lacks the integrations that a platform has. Knowing this, the Best-of-Breed provider can be on the front foot with Counter-Traps highlighting how they have all of the integrations the customer needs.

Better still, there is an opportunity for the Best-of-Breed provider to use this as an opportunity to lay a trap of their own. It could look something like:

"If you evaluate our competitors that offer a platform solution, they may tell you that we aren't integrated. The good news is that we have all of the integrations you need, AND because we are an open solution and not rigid

like a platform, we are likely to be able to integrate with any other solutions you bring on."

In this example, you have set a Counter-Trap that will defuse a trap you think your Competition will try to place, and you have set a trap of your own about your Competition's inflexibility to integrate other solutions.

Proof-Points - What points of proof do you have that highlight your strengths over your customer's and their weaknesses?

These could be customer references. Ideally, from customers in a similar sector with similar use-cases. You should highlight why they chose you and the positive results they have enjoyed since.

Education - Once you have completed your Competitive Strategy Plan, it is time to reflect on it and identify the parts you need to ensure that your Champion and other stakeholders are educated on. Another way of looking at this would be to consider if you were making an elevator pitch specifically to highlight your strengths over your Competition, then what elements would make it into your script?

While you are unlikely to share your Competitive Strategy Plan document with your customer, the process you go through as you initially build and evolve it over time will help you to focus on the parts of a Competitive Strategy that lead to success.

Having a Competitive Strategy Plan completed will arm you for any moment when you are put on the spot about your competition. You will be able to defend your value in the best manner, complete with all of the elements of your plan.

Competition and Procurement

Procurement is tasked with ensuring that their organization gets the best value for money. A major factor in this will be ensuring they pay what is perceived to be market rate or less. As most enterprise solutions don't have public pricing available, procurement has to rely on receiving multiple proposals from providers they perceive to be similar.

It is the Procurement team's prerogative to hold your competition's proposals next to yours. Being on the front foot in this instance is crucial, and following the procurement specific advice in the previous chapters will help ensure you engage with procurement in a good stance.

If you find yourself on the back foot and procurement are highlighting a cheaper competitor and using it to force you towards discounting in the first instance, you need to hold your ground firmly. If you have followed the advice in this book, you will have done too much good work to fall into the trap of discounting.

What to do if you find yourself on the back foot with procurement?

In the first instance, you should have your Champion supporting you through procurement, but if for any reason they aren't involved, the first thing to do is to try and level set with them.

Explain that you understand they are trying to find the best value for their organization. You can understand why they are drawing comparisons between the cost of your solution versus your competitors. However, you would kindly request that you focus on the value, rather than the price alone. Once you are permitted to do this, you need to take them through a high-level version of the Pain, Metrics, and how your solution aligns with the Decision Criteria.

When highlighting financial-based values, be sure to call out the predicted monetary amount of those values. Then, wrap up the overview by showing that your solution has come out on top throughout the Decision Process and how the process had highlighted the shortcoming of your competition's solution.

You may even want to summarize by breaking down the parts of your business case that showcase the predicted return on investment, particularly the areas of unique value.

Ideally, the unique value will be higher than the delta between the cost of your solution and your Competitors, which should help you eradicate the idea that your solution should cost the same as your Competition's.

Competition and your Sales Process

Your Competition is likely to play a part in your sales process, but hopefully not in the last stage!

Early-Stages:

Depending on how the customer's engagement has come about will dictate whether there is any Competition also engaged.

You should be looking to identify any Competition engaged, who they are, and what their sentiment is within the customer's organization. You should also be looking to establish whether there is an appetite to build your solution internally or whether any other projects or initiatives threaten your deal's priority.

Mid-Stages:

By the mid-stages, you need to have a full picture of who your competition is and how you stack up against them. You should not leave this to guesswork; you should get the answers to these questions from running your competitive intelligence against the Decision Criteria to see how you think the Competition scores before checking it with your Champion to get their perspective.

Your Champion's feedback at this stage is invaluable. You will need them to inform you where they think you and your Competition are both weak and strong and you need to build your Competitive Strategy with the information your Champion gives you.

By the later parts of the mid-stages, you should be leaning heavily into your Competitive Strategy. You should already be seeing the traps you've laid start to come to fruition.

Your Champion should be reporting back to you where you are making positive strides and working with you to overcome areas of your weakness.

Mid Consensus:

By the end of the mid-stage, you will want consensus that your solution is superior to your competition and that you are in a leading position in the Decision Process.

You should share this information with multiple stakeholders and, ideally, the Economic Buyer.

Late-Stages:

By the late stages, you should have a clear indication that you have the strongest solution. If you don't it is either because you are losing or you don't have a true Champion to inform you of your actual status. Both scenarios are problems that you should look to remedy immediately.

If you feel that your solution is seen as the superior and preferred solution, you will need to lean on your Champion to ensure that this message is shared to reach consensus across all stakeholders.

By the time your Paper Process is fully underway, your Competition should have been eradicated from your deal.

Summary Snapshot of in the sales process:

- Early: Is there Competition in this deal? Who is it?
- Mid: What is our competitive strategy? Is it working?
- Late: Are we a superior solution? Are we preferred / chosen?

Competition after you've won the deal

As most technology contracts have shifted from capital expenditure where the customer made large initial investments that then went onto represent sunken costs into a single solution, today, customers make smaller investments under an operating expenditure model. This means that a deal is never won forever, so it is vital that if you are victorious with your deal, you go on to deliver what you have promised and maintain a high standard of service.

Maintaining a high standard won't only secure the customer's business for the future, but it could also mean they go onto become a customer who can act as a reference which is particularly useful if you are competing with the same competitor in the future and they can come in and say "we picked you and we are glad we did".

Summary of Competition

Your Competition can be much more than just your rivals with comparative solutions. Your Competition can be other people internally fighting for the same resources either to build their own solution to the problem you solve or to invest in solving another problem altogether.

As a result of this complexity, it is essential that you quickly establish who your competition is and what the Political, Technical, and Commercial landscape with the Competition looks like.

Once you have a good handle on who your Competition is, you have to understand why your solution is better. Elite Sellers do this by digging in deep to the customer's Pains and needs using discovery find differentiators and Traps to set themselves apart.

Knocking the Competition directly will rarely have a positive outcome for the party being derogatory, and in some cases, it can backfire on them entirely.

Using a Competitive Strategy Plan can help keep all parts of a Competitive Strategy in focus and the Seller on the path to becoming the chosen vendor.

A word from Jack on Competition

"What you may notice about my thoughts on Competition is that they all revolve around your Champion. There's a good reason for that which is found in the third paragraph below." – Jack.

Use Your Champion and brief them like you are sending them into battle - Because you are! Your Champion is the person who is selling for you internally and defending your solution against FUD from Competitors and objections from those less informed.

Your Champion needs to be briefed about your solution and the competitive landscape that surrounds you.

The Strongest Champion Wins, not Vendor - When the decision comes to the Economic Buyer, they will pick the strongest Champion who may not necessarily represent the strongest solution.

Unlike technology, you can hold a Champion accountable, and this will reassure the Economic Buyer.

You'll have more than one competitive Champion - You already know that your Competition is more widely defined than just your rivals, as you will see other projects and initiatives compete against your solution too. Likewise, these different projects and initiatives will have Champions also.

What is your plan to help your Champion beat the Champion representing:

- Your Rival Solution?
- Another Project asking for the same Resources?
- Status Quo / No Decision?

RISKS

The Risks are the specific Risks that you have identified within your deal that will either remain and need to be monitored or overcome.

R isks can sit both with the Seller and the customer. A good example of a Risk is a deadline. For the Seller, a deadline could be the end of the quarter, whereas the customer may have a deadline relating to when they need your solution. Raising the awareness of a Risk like this will allow all parties to focus on finding ways to mitigate it.

Why I Added the R to MEDDPICC

I added the R for Risks to MEDDPICC when I led the sales team at Poq.

Poq is a SaaS company that makes apps for retailers. The biggest challenge they faced is that they are trying to create their own category.

The category is called App Commerce, and it represented native retail apps.

The best way to articulate the challenge that Poq had and why the Risk was such a factor when selling their solution is to look at the Three Whys:

Why should a retailer invest in having an app?

Why should they use Poq to build their app?

Why should they do this now?

If we go deeper into each Why you discover that each stage was fraught with Risk:

Major Risk 1: Why should a retailer invest in having an app?

There is a ton of pain around shopping on a mobile website. The experience is poor in comparison to an app. However, getting your customers to use your app is a challenge and requires substantial investment.

Major Risk 2: Why should they use Poq to build their app?

The most successful retailers all tended to build their apps and take control of the intellectual property themselves, so even though there was a compelling business case to partner with a software provider, the desire retailers had to own the app themselves often presented a significant Risk.

Major Risk 3: Why should they do this now?

An app for retailers fell most firmly under marketing technology, which at the last count had over 8,000 different solutions within its landscape.

As a Seller, if you had successfully passed the first two major Risks, you then had to face off with a multitude of other solutions that may have higher, or easier to attain returns.

This increased Risk in the sales process is on top of all of the usual Risks that can happen in a sales cycle, such as:

Unable to uncover meaningful Metrics

No access to the Economic Buyer

Decision Criteria is unknown, or we've failed to influence it

We don't know the Decision or Paper Process

The pain isn't significant, or we've been unable to implicate it

Unqualified Champion

Champion or other major stakeholder leaves or joins a different department

Our Competition has a more influential Champion than us

Our Competition has the march on us

While many sales organizations will call out these Risks within their appropriate sections of MEDDICC, given their importance, I like to call them out separately to focus on them.

The Levels of Risk

There are three levels of Risk in which we measure the severity in the form of a RAG Status (Red, Amber, or Green). Their definitions are loosely defined as:

- **Green Flag** - The Risk has either been overcome, no longer exists, or if it remains, it is confidently not seen as a Risk to the progression of the deal.

- **Amber Flag**- The Risk is not seen as a significant Risk, and it is not currently impacting the progress of the deal, although this may change. Efforts are ongoing to try and reduce the Risk.

- **Red Flag** - The Risk poses a significant threat to the success of the deal, and attempts to solve it should be undertaken urgently.

Examples of Risks

A Risk is anything that stands to threaten your deal's progression and just like Competition; they can fall into three categories:

- Political Risk
- Technical Risk
- Commercial Risk

A Competitor's particular strength could be a Risk, as could a shortfall of the functionality of your solution.

Risks could be related to more political or personnel matters such as a deadline you have before your Champion goes on maternity leave or leaves the business entirely.

On the Commercial side, you could experience Risk where your Competition has undercut your price so drastically that it may undermine your cost even if you have uncovered more value. Or you could have a scenario where the customer's legal team has raised a requirement that you know your company will have trouble accepting.

Risk and your Champion

Your best tool for eradicating Risks is your Champion. Not only can they give you more insights upon the challenge that is causing the Risk, but once you find a solution, you can send them in to bat for you.

Risk and The Go-Live Plan

There is a specific section within the Go-Live Plan which is devoted to highlighting any Risks.

The purpose of having this section within the Go-Live Plan is that it surfaces the Risks to the awareness of the customer.

Of course, you will only want to surface Risks that you want your customer to be aware of. For instance, you would be unlikely to highlight a Risk you have because of a weakness in your solution, but you are likely to highlight a Risk that the customer's legal team has created by demanding a term that you cannot accept.

You can also use this section to reinforce Risks that the customer faces themselves, such as a Risk around missing a deadline meaning they will miss the targeted Go-Live date or if they don't sign the contract by a specific time, a discount may be lifted.

Risks and your Sales Process

As your sales process evolves, so will the types of Risk that you are likely to face.

Early-Stages:

In the early stages of your deal, the Risks you face are likely to be related to the deal's qualification. A Risk is expected when you disqualify the deal and invest too much time into a deal that isn't winnable.

Fortunately, as an owner of this book, you now have a sales qualification methodology in your hands, which will help you to reduce this Risk.

Mid-Stages:

By the mid-stages, your deal should be fully qualified, meaning you have established that you have a fair shot of winning the deal.

You should have identified the majority of Technical Risks that you will be actively working to solve while trying to uncover any further Political and Commercial Risks that exist.

Late-Stages:

By the late stages of your deal, you should have all of the Risks surfaced and be actively trying to solve the ones you can.

Your Champion should be working closely with you to help you work through the Risks.

Summary of the Risks

Risks can pop up at any time during the deal. Unusually, a deal will exist without Risks. It is essential to uncover all Risks as swiftly as possible and plan to mitigate them.

LESSONS LEARNT WHILE IMPLEMENTING MEDDICC

I have worked in a variety of enterprise sales organizations from being the first employee at a company who didn't even have a product to Series A, B, C, D, and E startups, through to the behemoth that is Oracle where I was one of tens of thousands of Sellers.

Throughout this journey, I have seen a variety of deployments of MEDDICC from a 30-minute session as part of an onboarding plan presented by a sales administrator through to the most cost-intensive manner imaginable, including flying an entire sales team from all corners of the planet to Central America for a week-long training course.

I have seen firsthand the importance of the sales leadership team, and their level of adoption directly relates to the effectiveness of a MEDDICC deployment.

In my last two sales leadership roles, I have implemented MEDDICC as the first initiative I undertook upon starting the position. On both occasions, I had several initiatives I considered deploying, and on both occasions, MEDDICC was by far the most required initiative for me to implement.

In the first implementation, MEDDICC helped us control a sales organization that had no forecasting function at all. Further still, they called deals to close in weeks despite not having any communication from the customer for weeks. MEDDICC helped that organization achieve its annual target, which was a crucial requirement to help them towards their next fundraising milestone. This fundraiser gave us the ability to grow the sales team from 6 to 20 in 12 months and grow revenue by over 100% in the same period.

In my second implementation of MEDDICC, I took over responsibility for the EMEA region of a Series E startup with a commercial team of 16. Two years before I joined, the sales team had shifted from a mostly freemium model to selling paid plans. In the 12 months before I joined, they were beginning to focus upmarket towards the enterprise. By the time I joined, the focus was to shift entirely towards enterprise customers.

The EMEA region was lagging far behind the U.S., so much so that the U.S. sales team was twice as likely to win a deal compared to the EMEA, but on average, they would achieve more than twice as much revenue too.

Applying a strict focus on qualification via MEDDICC and an emphasis on going upmarket meant that within three quarters, we had doubled the average order value and reduced the average deal cycle time by 30%.

On this journey of various implementations of MEDDICC, I've learned some valuable lessons which I will share with you now:

1. You need to go all-in on MEDDICC

MEDDICC is binary. You either use it or you don't; there is no middle ground.

MEDDICC has to become part of the universal language in which your organization uses to talk about deals.

At the top of the funnel, the sales development team needs to be focused on identifying stakeholders such as Coaches, Champions, and Economic Buyers. Marketing needs to be using MEDDICC language to relate their initiatives to different contact types and the various stages of the sales process relating to MEDDICC.

Across the business's operations side, sales operations should embrace MEDDICC within their systems, such as the

CRM and any technology laid over the top of the sales process such as AI tools.

Existing processes need to shift to embrace MEDDICC; for example, QBR formats should be adapted to include MED-DICC language.

2. Front Line Managers are THE Most Important Adopters

The most significant factor to the success of your MEDDICC implementation lies in your front-line sales manager's hands. If they do not embrace MEDDICC in everything you do, your MEDDICC initiative will die.

Despite this, the front-line managers are rarely given the support they need to make MEDDICC a success. My advice for any organization planning on implementing MEDDICC would be that you spend two hours training the sales management team for every hour you plan to spend training Sellers on MEDDICC.

I'd strongly advise against undertaking any MEDDICC implementation initiative without a critical focus on training and supporting the first-line managers as a priority.

3. You Need the Full Support of the Executive Team

Find the world's fastest-growing enterprise technology companies, and you'll find MEDDICC. Look into their executive teams and you'll find other MEDDICC companies on their resume. Whether it's a CEO, CFO, or CMO, if they have worked with MEDDICC in one place, they'll want it in their next position. Why? Because MEDDICC means predictability and at C-Level being able to forecast accurately is invaluable.

If the executives at your company have worked with MED-DICC before, they will be very keen to support it being implemented into their current company. However, if they are new to MEDDICC, you will need to get their buy-in and executive sponsorship as it will be imperative to your implementation meeting its full potential.

To enact the kind of change management and adoption needed to embrace MEDDICC fully, you will need your executive team's support.

Sellers and sales managers are spinning so many plates that adding a new qualification methodology plate to their workload without top to bottom support stands the chance of being de-prioritized and subsequently fading away as just another failed initiative.

4. Celebrate and Showcase the Quick Wins

The beauty of MEDDICC is that when you overlay it over the top of a deal, it acts as a map. Often, without it, a salesperson is looking for the treasure (the deal), but they have no idea what route to go on to get it. MEDDICC marks the spot and uncovers the critical path you need to go down to get there. Before this, salespeople who haven't used MEDDICC should act as a EUREKA moment, like someone shining a light on their deal. It's essential to capture these moments and celebrate them to bolster support across your team.

Encourage a culture of MEDDICC celebration. Have you or someone in your team successfully qualified a Champion? Celebrate it! Have you obtained a consensus of the Decision Criteria? Celebrate!

Capture the moments in the deals where MEDDICC helped and reflect on them when you win. Likewise, if you qualify out based on MEDDICC, rejoice in the time you will have saved.

Celebrating and showcasing the wins helps to build visibility into the value of MEDDICC and subsequently will help you to gain traction upon its implementation.

5. Training Never Stops

Just like all parts of sales, you never stop learning with MEDDICC. Your peers, reports, and managers will also still have much to learn about MEDDICC.

Through researching and writing this book, I have spoken to those involved in creating MEDDICC, and those who've been using it for decades across multiple organizations. I have never come across a single person who felt they knew it all. Likewise, I can learn in an hour's conversation with an elite Seller like Lucy Williams-Jones than I did in over a year at a company that claimed to use MEDDICC but didn't embrace it.

To keep moving forward with MEDDICC, you have to continue using it, share your experiences with your peers, and seek advice from others around you.

Just as important as training, the existing teams on MEDDICC will be teaching MEDDICC to new employees. If you have an onboarding process, then MEDDICC must become a part of that. Better still is to build a certification of MEDDICC and how you use it for new starters to pass. This is useful even if the person coming in has used MEDDIC, MEDDICC, or MEDDPICC before, as you may well have a varied way of using it.

6 Run Mandatory MEDDICC Reviews

To accelerate the learning and adoption of MEDDICC, I recommend implementing mandatory weekly MEDDICC deal review sessions. Sellers are to bring a deal to the session to review with the team. You go through one deal a session and either ask Sellers to volunteer or run it via a rota.

Within the hour-long session, the Seller gives an overview of the background of their deal and a brief introduction of the organization they are selling to before going into each part of MEDDICC. The idea is for the team to review the deal and brainstorm strengths, weaknesses, and opportunities.

The sessions have a triple benefit:

1. The Seller whose deal is being reviewed gains the team's perspectives and will come out with a list of actions they can take to move their deal forward.

2. The team will learn from each other's experiences both concerning MEDDICC and from general selling skills, as well as industry or product-specific learnings.

3. The session represents a weekly engagement with MEDDICC that keeps it fresh in all your Sellers' minds. You can guarantee that while a colleague's deal is being reviewed, a Seller is considering MEDDICC against their own deal/s,

Another thing to consider with running MEDDICC reviews is to invite Sales Development Reps to the sessions. SDRs are often the talent of tomorrow, but it is a big step up to become a Seller, and there isn't much exposure they can get from the day to day development of deals. The MEDDICC sessions provide excellent exposure to the underlying workings of enterprise sales. Also, the more SDRs understand what makes a well-qualified deal, the more they can look for those signs when prospecting.

7a. Use MEDDICC Confidence Scoring to Focus on Progression

I found it useful to score each part of MEDDICC from one to ten based on each part's confidence level when reviewing a deal.

Scoring this way gives clarity over how much confidence we felt about each part. For instance, if we scored our Champion as a low score like one or two, we would know we needed to prioritize working on the Champion as an action following a deal review. Likewise, if there was a strong Competitor score, then we would know we need to focus on how we can tackle that as a priority.

If a Seller came into a MEDDICC deal review with a high score on the part of MEDDICC, it gave those conducting the review permission to dig deep to the part with the highest score to qualify the Seller's confidence and try to spot potential holes in their evaluation.

7b. Watch out for Happy Ears and the Pessimists

The challenge I quickly found with Confidence Scoring was that the scores would vary based on the buyer's optimism level. For instance, if a Seller had the common sales condition of 'HappyEaritus', a condition that affects the hearing of Sellers, meaning that they only hear good news and pro-actively ignore any bad news, they may score their MEDDICC higher than a pessimistic Seller.

Therefore, we implemented definitions and criteria for each level of scoring. For instance, on Metrics, a score of 1-3 would be:

1-3: We have an assumption of the Metrics based on outside information or initial conversations.

Whereas a score of 9-10 would be:

9-10: The customer openly uses our Metrics/the same Metrics in line with the objectives of the project, and they are the KPIs that will dictate the success of the project.

A fantastic by-product of MEDDICC Scoring is that if you implement the scoring into your CRM system, you can gain insight into the strengths and weaknesses of a deal at a glance. I am sure there are manners you can get more sophisticated by measuring scores across Sellers and improvements over time and where deals are stuck on low scores.

7c. Build MEDDICC into the sales stages

There are many organizations that have innovated with MEDDICC by doing things such as integrating it into their sales process and, subsequently, their CRM systems. There are several add-ons and standalone technologies that can help you integrate MEDDICC into your operations.

Using MEDDICC Scoring in the stages of your sales process, you can add a layer of qualification to your sales process. For instance, you may want to ensure that a deal can only pass to a late if it has a seven or higher Decision Process. The definition of a 7-8 Decision Process score is:

> *'We strongly understand the Decision Process the deal has to undergo and have qualified with our Champion that there are no other factors except those identified. We are aligned exceptionally close to the Decision Process. We have tested the accuracy of what we have been told through each stage and found it to be mostly accurate.'*

8. Marketing and MEDDICC

Brilliant marketing teams flank the world's best enterprise sales teams. As TripActions' CMO Meagen Eisenberg says that the CRO and CMO should become a 'Power Couple'.

MEDDICC and marketing can work well together for two main reasons:

1. Marketing can help drive progress on MEDDICC by running initiatives aimed at stakeholders like the Champion and Economic Buyer. Good examples of this are events such as Champion Building events or Round Tables designed at Economic Buyers. Another great initiative I have seen marketing do with MEDDICC in mind is to create content aimed at Economic Buyer personas such as the CFO. Documents like this can be used to open up conversations with Economic Buyers.

2. If the Sales team and Marketing team work closely together, then the Marketing team can benefit from hearing about real pains that are being uncovered by the Sellers in real-time. This can inform their marketing and help the Marketing team to produce more relevant content.

9. Don't Forget the Value

While MEDDICC is an outstanding qualification framework, it is not a replacement for a value selling framework.

If you are a Star Trek fan, think of the value selling framework as Captain Kirk, the charismatic leader, and MEDDICC as Spok, the logical sidekick. But if science-fiction analogies aren't for you, then let's stick with my earlier analogy of MEDDICC being Robin to the value selling methodology of Batman.

To sell your solution using the Metrics you have built, and against the Pain you have Implicated, you will need to translate your approach into value. A value framework is the best for this.

10. Always be Coaching

The first time I implemented MEDDICC into a sales team, I used to think I was a lousy teacher as it seemed no matter how many times I explained the same thing over and over, it didn't seem to resonate. An example of this would be where Sellers would describe their Metrics to me. They would just be the customer's internal Metrics for their business, completely unrelated to the solution, such as 'revenue' or 'users'. I would say time and time again:

"Metrics should be both specific to your deal and measurable. A good hack is to imagine we are going into a QBR with the customer six months after they've gone live and... What are the Metrics in which we would use to measure the success of our solution? Those are most likely your Metrics!"

Yet, week after week, I'd find myself repeating this.

I have come to learn that it isn't me and it isn't MEDDICC... it's just that Sellers and people generally have a lot going on, and they can't take it all in. So, always be coaching. Even if you think you sound like a broken record, if you are repeating yourself in response to improvements you want to see, you haven't repeated yourself enough!

MEDDICC CHECKLIST

Wouldn't it be easy to qualify your deals by simply 'checking' stages off of a checklist? Unfortunately, enterprise selling is far from being a linear process. If you are diving into this chapter hoping for a silver bullet qualification checklist, you will be disappointed. However, some parts of an enterprise deal can be checked against a checklist by asking questions such as:

Do I have a Champion?

- Have I qualified that they have power and influence?
- Have they shown that they are selling internally for me?
- Do they have a personal win relating to our success?

Questions like this should become a regular part of your qualification process, but due to how enterprise sales are rarely a linear process, it is hard to stay on top of what questions to ask and when.

This is where the MEDDICC Checklist comes in.

Checklists are used in industries where not just the complexity is at the highest level but also the stakes too. Such as in air travel and construction. When you take a flight and arrive safely at your destination, it is all because of the checks that have been completed against a checklist.

That said, not all high complexity and high stakes industries have always used a checklist. A surgeon called Atul Gawande found that half of all deaths in surgery were due to avoidable human error. He felt so passionately about this that he began to search for a solution. He found that in other high stakes industries, mistakes were avoided by using checklists.

Atul went on to take checklists back into the healthcare industry, and after three months of implementing checklists, significant complications in surgery had dropped by 36%, and deaths had dropped by 47%. Atul wrote a book on the subject called 'The Checklist Manifesto.'

If you are like me, when you read something educational like Atul's book, you relate it to your profession. As I was reading Atul's book, all I could think about was all of the times we in the sales profession could improve our forecast accuracy by implementing checklists. I have introduced two kinds of checklists to my sales teams. The first is a checklist to ensure we utilize the full strength of our go-to-market teams on deals we are engaged in. The checklist includes questions such as:

- Have we built a customized proposal?

- Have we engaged a potential reference to endorse us pro-actively?

- Have we engaged a co-founder or senior executive to contact the customer?

- Have we briefed our partner team?

The second checklist is focused squarely on qualification and how to put yourself into a position to be able to qualify. Not only to ask, is your deal qualified? But have you done the things that set you up to qualify the size of the opportunity? We know that completing a thorough discovery process is key to qualification, but have you done the right preparation to do a thorough discovery process? For example, have you:

- Read the customer's annual report and other public publications to reveal the customer's goals, challenges, and strategies?

- Have you mapped the customer's organization?

You know about the value of doing the things listed above, but do you do them every time? If not, why not? If you are like me, it is probably because you forgot or hadn't had the chance to plan the required preparation. This is where the checklist comes in and, in particular, the MEDDICC Checklist.

The checklist is constructed using the guidelines laid out by Atul Gawande and covers the main elements of an effective checklist:

Speed

An effective checklist has to be optimized to be efficient and fast to complete. Gawande says that a checklist should take less than 60 seconds to complete.

Pause Point

A Pause Point is an essential element as it represents the moment in which you pause to consider the item on the checklist.

A Pause Point could occur before you create an opportunity on your CRM system where you pause to check whether you have qualified that it is a valid opportunity. Other examples of potential Pause Points are:

- Before naming someone as your Champion, pause to check that you have qualified them as being a Champion

- Before sending over any pricing information for your solution, pause to check whether you have consensus of the value of your solution with your customer and have the appropriate engagement with the Economic Buyer.

The great thing about Pause Points in MEDDICC is that if you pause to check something that turns out to have a negative status, you can quickly adapt your actions to try and solve the state to be affirmative.

Killer Items

There should be 5-9 Killer Items on the checklist.

What defines a Killer Item is to reverse engineer what would happen if it was missed out. If it is likely that by missing this part of the checklist you would lose the deal, then it should be classed as a Killer Item.

An example of a Killer Item would be having a tested Champion or clarity of the Decision Criteria.

Complimentary to Expertise

The checklist is not designed to replace experience; it is intended to complement experience as a supplement to keep Elite Sellers focusing on the right things at the right moments.

Checklists are not about being robots; they are to help trigger a routine and formalize attention to detail instead of relying on your memory.

An Effective Checklist Requires Real-World Testing

If you don't already have a checklist, the MEDDICC Checklist is a strong starting point; however, to maximize the effectiveness of having a checklist, you should adapt it to suit the circumstances of your solution and industry. For instance, a Seller in Germany is likely to face more stringent technical and privacy requirements. The checklist should incorporate checks on this point, such as:

- Have we confirmed our privacy policy meets the levels of privacy illustrated in their Decision Criteria?

If you are thinking about introducing a checklist into your workflow, it is vital that you continuously test it and iterate it. A good starting point is to sit down with other Sellers within your organization and brainstorm what elements of your deals should be captured within a checklist.

A lot of the items you come up with will likely be the outputs of lessons learned the hard way. If you are struggling to think of things to add, then a good strategy is to analyze closed lost deals and reverse engineer what items you could have checked to identify issues earlier in the deal cycle.

Once you have your initial list, be sure to keep on iterating and find new items that should form part of the checklist.

-CUSTOMER LOGO HERE-

Notes

Meeting with Champion goals:
- Enable Champion to use our Metrics - re-introduce business case and ROI docs.
- Get Champion to set up meeting with Economic Buyer to introduce M2's. Brief Champion that we will intro CRO to EB.
- Send Decision Criteria ahead of meeting and ask Champion to confirm it on call and follow up with written confirmation request.
- Update Go Live Plan in real-time with Champion and ask for their input...
- Talk through Paper Process with Champion.
- Ask Champion "what happens for you when our solution is seen as wildly effective? Do you get a promotion? Bonus? - What is their personal win?!!
- Update from Champion on Competition. Get their buy-in to work on the Competitor strategy.

Metrics

Have we presented relevant Metric Proof Points (M1's)?

Have we transitioned to personalized Metrics for the customer (M2's)

Do we have a consensus on M2's?

Is our Champion using our Metrics?

Economic Buyer

Do we know who the EB is?

Have we engaged with them?

Are they aware of our M2's?

Have we aligned our senior execs?

Decision Criteria

Does the customer have an established Decision Criteria?

(if no) Are we working on helping the customer to build a Decision Criteria?

Have we confirmed the Decision Criteria in writing?

Do we have an active plan to stay on top of the Decision Criteria?

Decision Process

Do we know what the Decision Process is?

Have we transferred the Decision Process into a Go Live Plan?

Have we confirmed the Go Live Plan with the customer?

Does the customer buy into the Go Live Plan?

Paper Process

Do we know what the Paper Process is?

Have we confirmed it in writing with the Champion?

Have we transferred the Paper Process onto the Go Live Plan?

Have you specifically asked if there are any issues that could delay the Paper Process?

Implicate the Pain

Have we Identified the Pain?

Have we Indicated the Pain?

Have we Implicated the Pain?

Are we seeing urgency from the Pain?

Champion

Do I have a potential Champion?

Have I qualified that they have power and influence?

Have they shown that they are selling internally for me?

Do they have a personal win relating to our success?

Competition

Do I understand who my Competition is

Have we confirmed this with my Champion?

Have we built a SWOT analysis to fully analyze our position vs. our Competition?

Have we an effective strategy in place to get in front and stay in front of our Competition?

Closing Checklist

One of the highest value parts of the checklist is the Closing section. Like other industries, when the stakes go up, so does the value of the checklist, and if you are into the closing stages of your deal, then the stakes are at one of, if not the highest point.

In addition to the stakes being higher in the closing stages, the deal is likely to have evolved into a more linear process. Your success becomes less about the emotion of a decision and more about the steps towards completion.

The majority of these steps can fall under the Paper Process element of MEDDICC (or MEDDPICC as it would be).

An outstanding strategy to deploy with your Closing Checklist is to make it highly visible to the sales team. If you are within an office space, then whiteboards and dashboards work well. If you are a remote team, then surfacing the data online within a platform that is both easy to find and update is a good solution.

My recommended way of illustrating the Closing Checklist is to have the deals running along a Horizontal axis versus the stages to be checked upon the Horizontal axis.

It may look a little something like this:

Deal	Vendor of Choice	Verbal	Legal Engaged	Procurement Engaged	MSA	Order Form	Signer Engaged	Out of Office?	Go Live Plan	Agreed Date?
ACME	✓	✓	X	X	I.P	I.P	✓	✓	✓	X
Hooli	✓	✓	✓	✓	✓	✓	✓	✓	✓	✓
Umbrella	✓	X	X	X	X	X	X	X	✓	✓
Sterling Cooper	X	X	X	✓	X	X	X	✓	✓	✓
Initech	✓	X	✓	X	I.P	I.P	X	X	X	X
Wonka	X	✓	✓	✓	✓	X	X	X	X	X
Stark Inc	X	X	X	X	X	X	X	X	X	X
Soylent	✓	✓	X	✓	X	X	X	✓	✓	X
Wayne Enterprises	✓	✓	✓	✓	✓	✓	✓	✓	✓	✓

*'I.P' stands for 'In-Progress'.

The Closing Checklist breaks down the Paper Processes' known and unknown elements to ensure there are no surprises when managing the close.

In Summary

Implementing checklists into your selling will ensure you stay on top of all of the points you know are essential in your deal. A checklist should be seen as a complementary tool to a Seller's experience, and the most Elite Sellers embrace tools that improve their effectiveness.

To maximize the potential of a checklist, it is important that you personalize it to the specific requirements of your deals and continuously maintain and iterate it to retain its full potential.

MEDDICC SCORING

O nce you have successfully implemented MEDDICC into your selling, either as a Seller or to your team/organization as a Sales Leader, there are ways in which you can enhance how MEDDICC works for you and the first of those is to implement MEDDICC Confidence Scoring.

MEDDICC Scoring is a method to measure how confident you are about each part of MEDDICC. Each part is marked out of 10, with the objective being to get to 10, meaning the confidence on that part of MEDDICC is exceptionally high.

MEDDICC Scoring can be referred to on an ad-hoc basis on deals, or it can be implemented where MEDDICC is recorded, i.e., within the opportunity page on a CRM system.

Each scoring is split into four different definitions, with the lower two definitions having three scoring points across them and the higher two only having two scoring points per definition. This is because as the score gets lower, the definitions can be less specific, so it utilizes the additional scoring points to emphasize the stretch on confidence.

It is likely that your deal will commonly not match up with one exact scoring definition, and in these instances, you should select the score that feels like it best represents your confidence in that part of MEDDICC.

An important thing to note is that while the objective should be to raise each score towards a perfect ten continuously, Sellers should not be trying to falsely inflate their score or feel bad if they have a low score. A low score should be met with glee because it means that MEDDICC has fulfilled its purpose of uncovering an area that requires further qualification.

The scoring definitions of each part of MEDDICC are below:

Metrics:

1-3: We have an assumption of the Metrics based on outside information or initial conversations.

4-6: We have a reasonably good understanding of the Metrics based on specific conversations with the customer regarding the Metrics.

7-8: We strongly understand the Metrics driving the project, and we have communicated and confirmed these Metrics with at least two people within the customer's business. We have aligned ourselves to the Metrics.

9-10: The customer openly uses our Metrics/the same Metrics in line with the objectives of the project, and they are the KPIs that will dictate the success of the project.

Economic Buyer:

1-3: We have an assumption of who the Economic Buyer may be but we haven't had access to them yet.

4-6: We have confirmation of who the Economic Buyer is from our Champion/Coach, and they are aware of Our organization and our core value propositions. *Or* we have access to someone we think is the Economic Buyer but haven't had any confirmation.

7-8: We have had direct engagement with the Economic Buyer, and they are favorable to our solution.

9-10: We have a direct line of engagement to the Economic Buyer, and they are actively helping us to drive the progress of our deal.

Decision Criteria:

1-3: We have an assumption of the Decision Criteria for the project based on outside information or initial conversations.

4-6: We have a reasonably good understanding of the Decision Criteria based on specific conversations with the customer in regards to the Decision Criteria.

7-8: We strongly understand the Decision Criteria driving the project, and we have communicated and confirmed the Decision Criteria with at least two customers. We have aligned ourselves perfectly to the Decision Criteria.

9-10: We have confirmed, influenced, and documented the Decision Criteria with at least two major stakeholders (i.e., Economic Buyer & Champion), and they are completely aligned to it.

Decision Process:

1-3: We have an assumption of the Decision Process based on outside information or initial conversations.

4-6: We have a reasonably good understanding of the Decision Process based on specific conversations with the customer in regards to the Decision Process. We haven't been able to test the accuracy of the process against what we have been told.

7-8: We strongly understand the Decision Process the deal has to undergo and have qualified with our Champion that there are no other factors except those identified. We are exceptionally close to the Decision Process. We have tested the accuracy of what we have been told through each stage and found it to be mostly accurate.

9-10: We have written confirmation of the Decision Process from a senior stakeholder and are aligned perfectly with the process. We have been proactively introduced to parties relevant to each stage of the process (i.e., Technical, Legal, Procurement). We tested the accuracy of what we've been told through each stage and found it accurate.

Paper Process:

1-3: We have an assumption of the Paper Process based on outside information or initial conversations.

4-6: We have a reasonably good understanding of the Paper Process based upon specific conversations with the customer in regards to the Paper Process. We haven't been able to test the accuracy of the process against what we have been told.

7-8: We have fully vetted and confirmed the Paper Process with a major stakeholder within the organization and have been through a checklist of what needs to be completed and who is required for each step. We have been through all eventualities, including who is responsible for what, when, and where.

9-10: We have full commitment from our Champion and fully understand the critical path of how, where, and when each step will be completed. We will have tested this commitment and have had confirmation from the Economic Buyer to confirm what the Champion is telling us.

Implicate Pain:

1-3: We have an assumption of the pain based on outside information or initial conversations.

4-6: We have *Identified* a reasonably good understanding of the pain based upon a thorough discovery process with the prospect. We haven't been able to *Indicate* and confirm the severity or costs of the pain with other major stakeholders. We have aligned our values against the pain and have a good indication that they are understood.

7-8: The pain is well documented and has been *Implicated* throughout the customer's organization. They understand the cost of the pain and how progressing with our platform will eradicate that pain and the value that will be driven from it.

9-10: The Economic Buyer and Champion are actively aware of the pain and how we solve it. They have communicated this back to us and are actively talking about the pain and our solution internally to other stakeholders.

Champion:

1-3: We have a proposed Coach who has shown clear signs that they are favorable to us and is helping us to understand the lay of the land and progress the opportunity. We haven't tested whether they have power and influence, a vested interest in our success, or whether they are willing to sell internally.

4-6: We are confident that our Champion has power and influence and that they are pro-actively selling on our behalf, and we have tested them in doing so. We have tangible evidence that they are working as our Champion, and we can get time with them within a reasonable timeframe should we need it. Our Champion has come through when we've asked them for something (i.e., introduction to Economic Buyer, information about competitors or processes).

7-8: Our Champion is fast to update us on everything—good and bad! If the update isn't positive, they are working with us to counter any issues. They have shown a clear vested interest in our success.

9-10: Our Champion is actively campaigning for the success of our deal internally. They trust our advice on how to progress the opportunity and are proactive with helping us progress through each stage of the Decision Process and Paper Process.

Competition:

1-3: We have an assumption of who the Competition might be by outside information or initial conversations. We do not know where we stand against the Competition.

4-6: We have a reasonably good understanding of the Competition based on a thorough discovery process with the customer/accessing our network/information from our Coach/Champion. We haven't been able to confirm the Competition's proposition's strength, but we have laid some initial traps against them. We feel as though the customer favors our proposition.

7-8: We know precisely who the Competition is and what their proposition is. We have laid effective traps that we know have resonated via feedback from the customer. We do not feel exposed by their relationships, proposition, or commercials and have confirmation that we are the vendor of choice or are at least preferred.

9-10: We have eliminated the Competition from the deal. Except for a big change of circumstances, the customer is no longer considering any Competitors.

Risks:

Instead of scoring definitions for Risks, use flags.

Green Flag - There aren't any major Risks and / or any major Risks that have been solved / overcome.

Amber Flag - The Risks that remain are not major Risks and / or are being solved / overcome.

Red Flag - There is a Risk major enough to cause a threat to the deal's success, and attempts to solve or overcome it should be undertaken urgently.

EPILOGUE

MEDDICC isn't a dirty little secret

One thing that always surprises me about the sales industry is just how ashamed many salespeople are to admit they are in sales. Many Sellers will do everything they can to avoid affirming to the customer that they are, in fact, a salesperson.

I have news for you—customers know you are a Seller. They even know you want to sell to them! Yes! Even if you have a spruced-up title!

My advice is to lean into sales. You aren't fooling anyone by pretending to be a 'consultant'; even if you are, is that the outcome you want? Do you want to set the expectation that your engagement with the customer is all about giving them free advice? What does that say to them about how you perceive your value?

If you approach every sales engagement with the mentality of: 'I only invest my time and expertise into engagements where the customer is considering my services', then you will win far more deals than the odd one you win by somehow luring the customer into a false sense of security of you not being there to sell to them, so you can surprise them with an order form, which, of course, they'll sign immediately because, you know... "GOTCHA!"

Most sales professionals know that the best way to align themselves with their customers is to align their sales process to their customer's buying process. MEDDICC is the ideal methodology to empower that.

Imagine for a moment that your sales manager is a stickler for MEDDICC, and you have an upcoming deal review with him / her where he/she is likely to go deep on MEDDICC. In preparation for the review, you realize you have many unanswered questions about every aspect of MEDDICC, so in a moment of panic, you call your Champion and ask for the answers:

You: "Hey, Charlie, I've got it down here that Eve is the Economic Buyer on this deal?"

Charlie Champion: "She's the what?"

You: "Sorry... I mean, she's the one who approves the budget."

Charlie Champion: "Well, yeah, it's my budget, but she has to sign it off."

You: "Right, so even if you said you wanted to do this, she could still block it?"

Charlie Champion: "Yup."

You: "Ok, thanks. What about the Decision Process? As I understood it, the RFP answered all of the preliminary factors you had considered from a technical perspective. Are there any more steps ahead of us that we need to go through to get technical validation?"

Charlie Champion: "Yes, a few, they are..."

This is an extreme example. Your motives for obtaining this information should be your deal's success, not to appease your boss. Still, it shows that even if you purely seek to get a deeper understanding of MEDDICC on a deal directly with a client, they are likely to answer affirmatively.

Once again, if your customer is unwilling to share necessary information on how you can both get a deal done together, these are big red flags that should concern you about the health of your deal and how well it is qualified.

The message I want you to get from this chapter and, more specifically, this book is that MEDDICC is a methodology that will help you to become a more successful version of yourself. You will be more efficient and more outcome-driven.

By embracing MEDDICC in every element of your sales process and pro-actively using it at every opportunity, you will find yourself firmly on the front foot.

APPENDIX

Other Types of Qualification Methodology

CHAMP

CHAMP differentiates itself over BANT because it focuses on the Challenge (CH) first. From there, it is pretty similar to BANT.

The A stands for authority as it does in BANT.

The M stands for Money, which is the same as Budget in BANT.

The P is for Prioritization, which is Timing in BANT.

Part of me wonders whether CHAMP would exist if it didn't sound better than NATB, which is BANT re-ordered to follow the process as CHAMP says it should be done.

My perspective is that you shouldn't be linearly following any qualification acronym anyway as it won't be a pleasant experience for the customer who will feel like they are being pushed through a scripted process.

GPCTBA/C&I

I debated putting this framework in the book because I envisaged someone picking the book up at the bookstore and skimming to this page and thinking that there was some glaring typo. Believe it or not, GPCTBA/C&I is a genuine framework (and not created by a cat walking across someone's keyboard).

It was developed within HubSpot and stands for: Goals, Plans, Challenges, Timeline, Budget, Authority, Negative Consequences, and Positive Implications.

What I like about GPCTBA/C&I is that by the very nature of the number of information elements it needs, it is likely that Sellers will be taking GPCTBA/C&I further than the initial engagement.

What I don't like about GPCTBA/C&I is that it doesn't do too much more than BANT in terms of qualification. The Goals, Plans, and Challenges can all be covered by Need in BANT. The Budget and Authority are the same, and the Negative Consequences and Positive Implications fit less into qualification and more into part of a sales methodology or value framework.

HubSpot has enjoyed incredible success and has been led by some of the sharpest sales leaders in the business, and this framework has been designed to suit both their type of customer and how they sell.

While it does go further into the sales funnel than most other qualification frameworks, it doesn't tackle any of the qualification criteria relating to the customer's process of how they get a deal done internally and how you as a Seller can plan and align with that. For this reason, this framework still leaves a lot to be desired for enterprise selling.

FAINT and ANUM

FAINT (Funds, Authority, Interest, Need, and Timing) and ANUM (Authority, Need, Urgency, Money) are just variations of BANT. Again, these frameworks emphasize BANT's shortfalls in terms of the order of the acronym, although FAINT is pretty much identical except for emphasizing Interest separately from Need.

Qualify to the End

On the one hand, it is good to see so much consistency across the five alternative qualification frameworks to MEDDICC, as listed above. Fundamentally, they all focus on finding Budget/Money/Funds, Authority, Need/Interest/Goals/Plans/Challenges, and Timing/Urgency.

However, on the other hand, none of these solutions are fit for anything else in enterprise sales except for early qualification by the SDR before passing the opportunity over to the Seller, as once a deal passes through the qualification criteria as set out by these frameworks, the deal is going to be off the rails in terms of qualifying the following key elements:

- Metrics - What are the Metrics that the decision-making committee is going to use to evaluate your solution's value? Do we have them? Are they strong enough?

- Economic Buyer - While Authority may help identify who has the authority, it leaves an opaque view of who is who. With most Authority-based strategies, all roads lead to the Champion and qualifying if they have authority.

- Decision Criteria - What is the Criteria that the customer uses to base their decision on? How do you score against it? Should you be in this deal?

- Decision Process - The big one that is missing along with the Paper Process. What are the stages ahead, and how can you set yourself up to accelerate through the process? This is much more than just a timeline of events; it involves stakeholders, third parties, dependencies, and more.

- Implicate the Pain - You could argue that Pain is well covered within Need/Interest/Goals/Plans/Challenges, but in MEDDICC, it is much more than just about Identifying the Pain. It needs to be implicated upon the customer, so they feel the scale of the problem they have.

- Champion - Generally, the Champion is covered by Authority, which usually focuses on testing the Champion's power and influence within their organization.

- Competition - None of the above qualification frameworks pay any attention to Competition. Neither did the original version of MEDDICC when it was created decades ago. But qualifying your Competition's position in your deal in the early stages and maintaining a focus on qualifying their position throughout is a critical element of MEDDICC.

With the qualification frameworks above, you are effectively on your own once you pass your deal's early stage. This puts a considerable Risk on your forecast as enterprise deals change in shape and size throughout their lifecycle. What was once qualified as any part of BANT or its variations becomes outdated or irrelevant, particularly as you move throughout the Decision Process and into the Paper Process.

REFERENCES

Blair Warren, The Forbidden Keys to Persuasion, page 39

Chris Voss, 'The Art of Letting Other People Have Your Way' The Knowledge Project Podcast, page 79, 118

Atul Gawande, The Checklist Manifesto, pages 244-246

John Kaplan, President of Force Management, B2B Growth and Strategy Consultancy, Pages 5, 12, 89,122, 129,

Force Management, B2B Growth and Strategy Consultancy http://www.forcemanagement.com, Pages 5, 13, 17, 18, 33, 89, 122, 129, 181,

Neil Rackham, Spin Selling, pages 9, 33, 181

Jack Napoli, Sales MEDDIC Group, pages 4, 10-17, 20, 83, 113, 123, 141, 159, 169, 177, 186, 210, 227

Sales MEDDIC Group, pages 33, 83, 113, 123, 141, 159, 169, 177, 186, 210, 227

Roy T. Bennett, The Light in the Heart, page 65

Theodore Roosevelt, Theodore Roosevelt on Bravery: Lessons from the Most Courageous Leader of the Twentieth Century", page 66